D0090049

UNITED WE STAND

HOW WE CAN TAKE BACK OUR COUNTRY

ROSS PEROT

 HYPERION NEW YORK

ISBN 1-56282-852-5

10 9 8 7 6 5 4 3

Contents

This book is dedicated to the millions of volunteers who accomplished the seemingly impossible task of getting the petitions signed. You did it brilliantly.

You changed American politics in just five months.

You made it clear that the people, not the special interests, own this country.

Everyone in Washington now understands that the American people own this country, have reasserted their roles as owners, and want the country's problems addressed and solved.

The creativity, ingenuity, and focused dedication to this task are unique in American politics.

The founders of our government must be looking down from heaven, smiling on all of you.

Acknowledgments

For years I watched with concern as the national debt mounted and our competitive position declined. I collected news items, government reports, outside critiques, and editorial opinions that told the story step by step and instance by instance. I listened to thousands of people in and out of government. These people have good, solid, practical ideas about how to solve our country's problems and put it on the right path.

To all of you who gave me ideas and plans, I offer my thanks. If the content of this book seems familiar, it is because your ideas are valuable and deserve to be studied carefully.

To the team that assembled these ideas into a workable framework I owe a debt of gratitude, especially to: John White, Bob Peck, Richard Fisher, Doug Austin, Steve Brooks, Carol Cimitile, Cathy Eddy, Eric Hoffmann, Mia Lee, Steve Ostrover, David Parkhurst, Susan Bruns Rowe, Laura Sainz, Kevin Warmath, and Andrew Wise. I'm especially grateful to Ashley Chaffin, whose ability to track down any fact or answer any question is first-rate.

Thanks to Tom Luce, David Bryant, Brad Harris, and Clay Mulford for their observations, comments, and help.

I told the American people I would study the issues and tell them my positions on matters that will determine our country's future.

ACKNOWLEDGMENTS

This book and the movement that spawned it are only the beginning. I urge you to continue to monitor your government and to demand results from all candidates and officeholders, especially in this election year. Only the people can rebuild America.

UNITED WE STAND

Introduction

Unless we take action now, our nation may confront a situation similar to the Great Depression—and maybe even worse. Our economic growth has been sluggish for nearly two decades. The unemployment numbers remain depressing, while the Federal Reserve worries about inflation.

The institutions we depend on to preserve our financial security are shaky. If they fail, millions of people will be devastated. Banks are already weak. The Federal Deposit Insurance Corporation (FDIC), which we as taxpayers guarantee, may incur liabilities greater than those from the recent Savings & Loan crisis.

In other words, our economy is perched on the edge of a cliff. Either we work together to climb back to safety, or we must brace ourselves for potential disaster. This book provides a plan to pull our nation back from the brink. It is the legacy of a movement unparalleled in American history.

I look at this book as a dynamic plan that will stimulate discussion and debate. The only objective is to create the plan that best serves the American people, and then implement it! We want action, not words.

Not everyone who supported me or participated in this great movement will agree with everything I write. I am only one voice in a loud chorus. I do hope that people who agree with me about the symptoms of our national disease, even if they dispute some of my proposed cures, will use this book as a means of judging candidates for national office in the November elections.

In the space of six months, the grassroots movement roused the nation and shook the political establishment to its core. They did it working as a team. That's why they call themselves United We Stand. The result is that candidates for President, Senate, and House of Representatives are listening to the people as they haven't done in years. This movement will succeed if it holds the candidates accountable. Ask them specific questions, and require specific answers: What about the deficit? What about entitlements? What about the special interests? What about foreign governments hiring American lobbyists to write our laws? What about our government's hobbling of business? What about our loss of jobs to foreign countries?

Washington has created a government that comes *at* us instead of a government that comes *from* us. Slick campaign commercials and entertaining television spots won't work in 1992 if *you* ask the questions and demand the answers.

You are the owners of this country. Nobody else can do the job. Our system has been corrupted because we weren't exercising our responsibilities as owners.

This is the year to reassert your ownership.

One voice is tiny, and alone it cannot be heard above the din of politics as usual. The people's voice, when it cries as one, is a great roar. United We Stand: that's the magic. It cannot be ignored.

You can change our country.

You can pass on the American dream to our children.

You can change the world.

CHAPTER ONE

An America in Danger

I n June, 117,000 more Americans were thrown out of work. While we were putting the finishing touches on this book in July, eight companies announced they were shedding 23,000 jobs. Those were just the *announced* layoffs.

The Federal debt is now $4 trillion. That's $4,000,-000,000,000. Our political leaders will add over $330 billion to that debt in 1992 alone.

We add about $1 billion in new debt every 24 hours.

Does anyone think the present recession just fell out of the sky?

People are working longer and longer hours to accomplish less and less. New families can't afford to buy their first homes. In many families, both parents must work to make ends meet. Young people coming out of high school or college can't find a job, so even more of a burden is carried by the families that raised them.

If your family is fortunate enough to have had a child or grandchild born in 1992, by the time that child enters the third grade in the year 2000 the Federal debt could be double what it is today.

Let's try to imagine that third-grade classroom just eight years from now.

Today we have a $4-trillion debt. By 2000 we could well have an $8-trillion debt. Today all the income taxes collected from the states west of the Mississippi go to pay the *interest* on that debt. By 2000 we will have to add to that all the income tax revenues from Ohio, Pennsylvania, Virginia, North Carolina, New York, and six other states just to pay the interest on the $8 trillion.

If you live in one of those states, take a look at the IRS payroll deduction that reduces your next week's take-home pay. Your money is going just to pay interest on this debt, which in 1993 will amount to $214 billion. During the first 152 years of our nation's existence, we spent less than $214 billion to operate the entire government of the United States!

Think of the Louisiana Purchase, the westward expansion, the Civil War, Reconstruction, the building of the railroads, the assimilation of millions of immigrants, and the industrialization of our economy. All the great achievements that built America into the world's most dynamic and powerful nation were accomplished without any substantial debt.

And let me repeat: that $214 billion we'll pay next year is interest only. Interest doesn't buy a thing. It doesn't spur new business to give people jobs. It doesn't

AN AMERICA IN DANGER

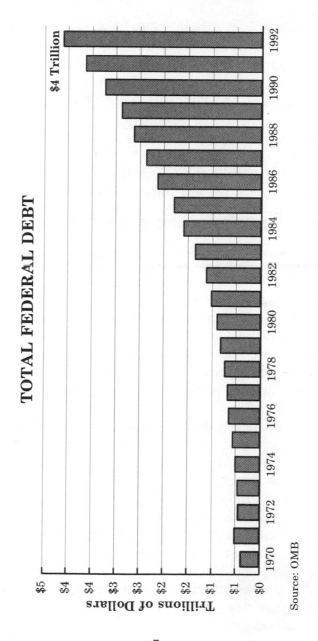

TOTAL FEDERAL DEBT

Trillions of Dollars

$5 $4 $4 $3 $3 $2 $2 $1 $1 $0

$4 Trillion

1970 1972 1974 1976 1978 1980 1982 1984 1986 1988 1990 1992

Source: OMB

help people out of poverty. It doesn't maintain our highways. It doesn't protect our forests and national parks. It doesn't put more police on the streets. It doesn't restore our inner cities. It doesn't defend us. It will never build a classroom or fund research to fight disease.

The debt is like a crazy aunt we keep down in the basement. All the neighbors know she's there, but nobody wants to talk about her. If we allow the debt to grow, however, we are impoverishing ourselves. An $8-trillion debt would be a disaster requiring us to overtax our people, slash services, and severely reduce pensions and Social Security.

We are a great nation. We are a people with a great heart. We want to reach out to the single mother struggling to support herself and her children. We want to help the disadvantaged, provide scholarships for deserving students, and make basic health care available to anyone who needs it. Instead, the result of the toil, sacrifice, and dedication of our working people will go into paying the interest on a government debt we shouldn't have created in the first place.

Elected officials don't like to talk about what that massive runaway debt is doing to our country. Instead they keep to the time-honored tradition that has become standard for our elections. They talk about every tiny group's special interest and do nothing about an economy in sharp decline.

This year it *must* be different. The movement to place my name on the ballot has accomplished a major goal. It has focused the nation's attention on the real problems facing our country. Instead of swatting flies in the kitchen and stomping on ants in the living room, this year the nation will focus on the gorilla charging up the front steps—the debt.

We have to face up to our debt. We have to do it now. We have to do it because no nation can afford to pay $214 billion a year for nothing. We have to do it because what happens in that third grade classroom eight years from now will determine the future course of American history.

How Bad Is It?

Not only have the politicians failed to reduce the deficit and the interest we pay on it, in 1992 alone we will add over $330 billion to the $4 trillion we've already piled on our children's shoulders. That doesn't include another $3 trillion in the form of money the government has already promised to spend in the future. Our leaders keep those liabilities off the books. The weight of that debt may destroy our children's futures.

Suppose the American people demanded radical action tomorrow to eliminate just this year's addition to the debt. We've seen much posturing recently about a Constitutional amendment to balance the budget. Suppose we decided to take one action this year to wipe out this year's deficit and balance the budget. Here are some radical but unrealistic choices to show just how big the deficit is:

- Shut down the Defense Department. Abolish the entire army, navy, and air force. That wouldn't be enough to erase $330 billion of new debt.

- Shut down all the public schools nationwide. That would get us $330 billion.
- Seize the profits of all the Fortune 500 companies. That doesn't get us even half of what we need.
- Confiscate the wealth of the Forbes 400, the richest people in the nation. That wouldn't do it either.
- Now for the worst option: raise everyone's taxes. How much would we have to raise income taxes on every person in the United States just to eliminate this year's deficit? We'd have to almost *double* them!

That's how big a $330-billion deficit is, and we haven't even begun to tackle the $4 trillion we already owe.

How Did It Happen?

How did one year's deficit become so large? How did things get out of control?

In 1990, George Bush and the Democratic leadership made a deal. The President backed off of his pledge of "no new taxes" and agreed with Congress to raise taxes by $166.5 billion. We were told we would have a budget deficit of only $96 billion. That's still a lot of new debt, but it was a major step in the right direction.

So we all went along.

There were secrets in that budget agreement neither the President nor the members of Congress of both parties who approved it told us about. Specifically, there were authorizations for $304 billion in *new* spending—$1.83 in new spending for every dollar they raised in new taxes.

AN AMERICA IN DANGER

Instead of the $96-billion deficit we'd been promised, Washington was "shocked" to discover a few months later that the deficit would really be $318 billion. A little while later, they raised the estimate yet again.

President Reagan had a reason for the deficit spending that occurred in his Administration. He wanted to bankrupt the Soviet Union, and he did it by accelerating the arms race. In the last several years, our debt has grown for no reason. Government spending has risen to a record 25 percent of our gross national product, and it hasn't bought us much.

The United States is the largest and most complex business enterprise in the history of mankind. Elected officials like to say that government can't be run like a business. I can see why. In business, people are held accountable. In Washington, nobody is held accountable. In business, people are judged on results. In Washington, people are measured by their ability to get reelected. With 96 percent of Congress reelected in 1990, they must be running the most successful enterprise in the world, and they reward themselves handsomely for it.

Let's bring it down to the level of a small town. Let's assume in this small town there has always been one person who has been generous and helpful and caring all his life, as our country has been. Suddenly he finds that he's bankrupt from making bad investments and running up too much debt. Can he still give to the United Way? Can he give to the Salvation Army? Can he endow the community college or donate food to the homeless shelter or help build a new house of worship? Can he help anyone anymore? No, he can't. And what's worse, *he's* the one who now needs help.

Will that be our country's fate? Is that what all the

dreams and hopes of two centuries will come to? Is that why our mothers and fathers labored or why our soldiers died, so that the greatest country the world has ever known would come to this?

An America that Worked

We used to be the country that did things no one else could do. We created the cotton gin, and clothed the world. We created the harvester, and fed the world. We created the electric light and turned night into day. We taught the world how to fly. We invented the telephone. After a French company tried and failed, we went and built the Panama Canal.

The integrated circuit is one of our country's great inventions—created and first manufactured in America. Yet, 19 out of 20 integrated circuits used in the United States today come from Japan.

After World War II, Japan and Germany lay in ruins. Today they are economic superpowers. In 1946, Humamatsu Honda was wandering around the streets of Tokyo looking for scrap iron to make a motor scooter. Today his company's profits are over $1 billion a year. In 1951, Toyota was bankrupt. Today it is the third largest car maker in the world. Toyota City, Japan—not Detroit, Michigan—is the car capital of the world.

Did they discover a secret? No. There's no secret. They made the hard choices; our leaders made the easy ones. For their sizes, Germany invested over twice as much, and Japan invested over three times as much as we did throughout the 1980s to build their countries. Our political and business leaders seem to think short term. Their leaders think long-term.

Before the early 1970s, our standard of living doubled every generation and a half. Now it will take *twelve* generations for our standard of living to double! This is not the America our parents and grandparents knew.

We've allowed ourselves to be lulled into thinking that the bills would never come due. We've been led to believe we could keep on borrowing our children's money to finance a lifestyle we haven't earned and can't afford. It can't go on.

Betrayal by the Elites

After taxes, the average household income in the Washington, D.C., area is the highest of all major metropolitan areas, especially in the surrounding bedroom communities of Washington where our political elites live.

How come?

Who are these people who make these big salaries and what do they do to earn them?

These are the people who go to Washington to do good and stay to do well for themselves. They take government jobs to gain expertise and add to their resumes. Then they use what they learned on our payroll to grab $500,000 consulting contracts from foreign governments and big interests. This is the famous revolving door.

The revolving door is truly bipartisan. Members of Congress, top congressional aides, cabinet members, aides to the President, and campaign officials are very

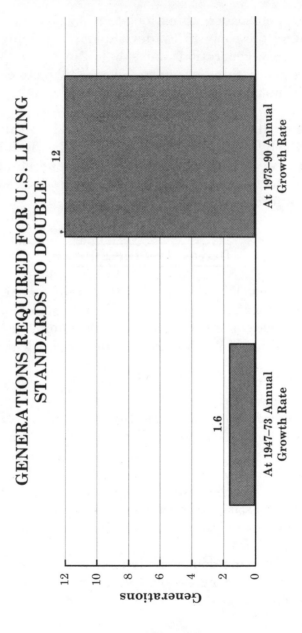

GENERATIONS REQUIRED FOR U.S. LIVING STANDARDS TO DOUBLE

12

1.6

At 1973–90 Annual Growth Rate

At 1947–73 Annual Growth Rate

Generations

12

10

8

6

4

2

0

happy to join hands across the aisle if it will help in the scramble to represent the big interests with big budgets to spend. You've seen them swarming at the national conventions where "hospitality" is often a polite word for something else.

I'd like you to ask two simple questions: First, what are they selling? Second, who needs to buy what they're selling?

To get the picture, look at the system they've created. Elections have become so expensive that our elected representatives spend most of their time raising money from special interests to finance their campaigns so they can get back into office. When they're back, they raise *more* money to get reelected again and again. A lobbyist walks in the door with a fat check from the special interest political action committee (PAC) he represents. If you were that elected official, you would listen carefully to what he has to say. Pretty soon, the elected person doesn't have time for his own constituents. He needs to spend his time listening to these people who give him the money to stay in office.

If you ever have a chance to visit Washington, drop in on that elected official. Chances are he won't be able to see you. He's too busy.

It wasn't always this way. When I was a midshipman in the Naval Academy, my folks and I paid a visit to Washington to see the sights. While we were touring Capitol Hill my mother decided she wanted to visit one of the senators from Texas. Here we were, a common family from Texarkana, and we walked into a senator's office and said we were from Texas and wanted to meet our senator. Five minutes later we were ushered into the office of Lyndon Johnson, majority leader of the

United States Senate. Don't bother trying that today.

It's easy to see what the Washington lobbyists, political consultants, and lawyers are selling to their clients. They're selling the access you aren't allowed anymore. They make their living by "providing access."

Who are the buyers?

More and more, foreign governments and businesses are the buyers. If you wonder why international trade is not played on a level playing field, don't point a finger at the Japanese or the British or anyone else. Look first at our own political elites who enter government to gain expertise and personal contacts while on the public payroll, then leave to enrich themselves by taking inside knowledge to the other side. We've had American trade negotiators quit on Friday and show up on Monday as consultants for the country they were just negotiating with. What has happened to common decency, ethics, and patriotism among the people who are supposed to lead our country?

Who's to Blame?

Whenever a citizen raises questions about the conduct of our government and its officials, our representatives look around for someone to blame. Whenever a voter asks an embarrassing question about the decline of our economy, the first reaction is to blame someone else. The President blames Congress, and Congress blames the President. Republicans blame Democrats, Democrats blame Republicans, and both of them blame the bureaucracy. The bureaucracy has caught on, too. Last year when the budget projections were wrong, the Office of Management and Budget (OMB) actually blamed the Department of the Treasury, as if Treasury was some mysterious organization located in Mongolia.

Modern politics has become little more than shirking responsibility and blaming somebody else. There is, however, a very obvious answer to this.

If anyone wants to know who's to blame for the $4-trillion debt, just go look in the mirror.

You and I are to blame. You and I are the shareholders of this country. We own it.

We allowed this system to develop where political action committees, the tools of the lobbyists, have more power than people. We allowed politicians to buy our votes by promising newer and grander giveaways (with money, by the way, they didn't have and had to borrow from our children). We allowed them to rack up deficit after deficit while we reelected them time after time.

As owners, you and I established the incentives. How could we be surprised at the results?

Why do we find it strange that the Senate voted itself a 23 percent pay increase last year after it had just approved the largest deficit in American history? Did *you* get a 23 percent increase last year? Do you know anyone who did? Our senators only did what they thought we would let them do. They blamed that deficit on somebody else and got on to the really important business of taking care of themselves. We did exactly what they expected us to do: nothing.

You and I didn't start this country; we didn't build it. Only a few of us have done anything to deserve or preserve it. We inherited our ownership stock.

We were given only one charge by the generations

UNITED WE STAND

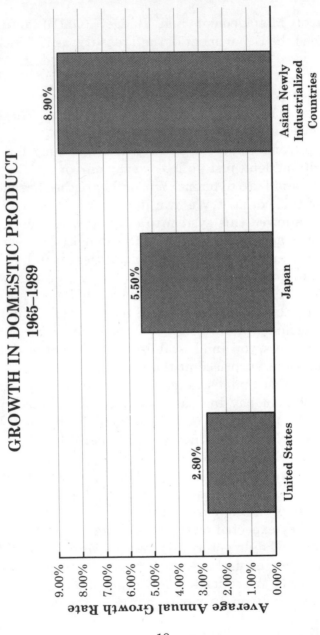

GROWTH IN DOMESTIC PRODUCT
1965–1989

18

AN AMERICA IN DANGER

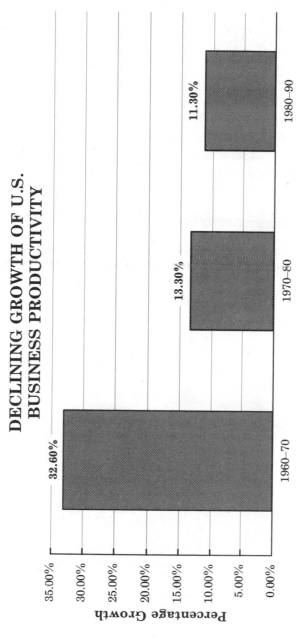

DECLINING GROWTH OF U.S. BUSINESS PRODUCTIVITY

32.60% 1960–70

13.30% 1970–80

11.30% 1980–90

Percentage Growth

35.00% 30.00% 25.00% 20.00% 15.00% 10.00% 5.00% 0.00%

who left it to us. We were to do as they did and pass this nation on to our children in better shape than they left it to us.

Who among us in good conscience is willing now to say that this solemn charge has been fulfilled? Which ones of us loves their country or children or grandchildren so little that they would leave behind an America weaker or sicker than the one they inherited? Who among us can look at these facts and turn away with a shrug?

These are not simple problems that can be solved with a single vote on Election Day. One person in one office will not restore excellence to America.

There is only one person in the entire world who can with character, devotion, hard work, and sacrifice create an America stronger and healthier than it is today.

Go back and look in that mirror again.

CHAPTER TWO

An America that Reforms Its Politics

Our political system has lost its moorings. It no longer rises to meet new challenges.

It seems designed to avoid solving problems.

The first words of the Constitution are "We, the people." *We* created the Constitution. *We* created Congress. It exists for us, not the other way around. *We* hire and pay for the bureaucracy. *They all work for us.*

Before we can hope to face up to our problems, we have to restore the intent and meaning of the Constitution we created. We cannot repair our economic engine, retool our economy to be competitive in a new age, and put ourselves on a solid footing for the future unless we take back control of our government that has been taken from us.

The first and most important action we can take as a people is to treat our elections seriously. Candidates for public office must be required to lay out their proposed solutions to the problems that confront us. They avoid this like the plague. They'll raise false issues, appeal to the voters' self-interests, or sling mud—anything to avoid facing the tough issues.

The Savings & Loan crisis is a case in point. In 1984, the administration and Congress believed that the S & L crisis was a $20- to $30-billion dollar problem. The special interests mobilized. The S & L operators flooded Washington with lobbyists, campaign contributions, PAC money, and free airplane trips to fancy resorts. As a result, the issue was swept under the rug. It didn't reappear on the screen during the 1988 elections. The day *after* the 1988 election, our Republican President and Democratic Congress suddenly discovered we had a $400- to $500-billion S & L crisis that could no longer be ignored.

In 1990 we were told by Washington that the deficit for the next five years would be $547 billion. A year later we were told there was a slight mistake. The five-year deficit would total $1 trillion. As usual, nobody wanted to talk about it.

Do not allow any candidate in this election to ignore our deficit. When Governor Clinton talks about his new programs, ask him where the money is coming from. When President Bush talks about finishing the job he started, ask him when he's going to start on the job of getting this country back on track. If you will hold all the candidates accountable, then we'll be on the way to getting this problem fixed. You will have done your part no matter for whom you vote.

AN AMERICA THAT REFORMS ITS POLITICS

After the election the real work will begin. The men and women who are chosen by the people to go to Washington in 1992 should pledge themselves to restore the people's control over our institutions. That will mean irritating their powerful friends and big donors. It will also mean shutting the revolving door. It will mean restoring the intent of the Constitution.

Start at the Top

Before we can hope to eliminate our deficit, we have to overhaul the political system that created it. Our Founders built a beautiful ship of state, but the barnacles have latched on and the hull has rusted. It's time for a scrubdown from top to bottom.

It's not just a matter of bringing in new people. It's not just a matter of replacing a Republican President with a Democrat, or a Democratic Congress with a Republican one. To throw the rascals out is an impulse as American as apple pie, but it alone won't do the job.

The wave of new members of Congress who were elected in 1974 as reformers in the wake of the Watergate scandal were as bright and sincere as Congress has ever seen. Eighteen years later those who remain in office are as encrusted in the system as the people they replaced. They enjoy the same perks, PAC payouts, bounced checks, fawning staffs, and personal exemptions from the laws they pass.

Take any good, decent citizen and put him in a limousine, hold the red lights for him, give him a private jet for personal use, supply him with free tickets to any place he wants to go, and he'll lose touch with reality in a hurry. If we replace every person in Washington tomorrow but keep the present system intact, in a few weeks the new people will be just like the old people.

The British aristocracy we drove out in our Revolution has been replaced with our own version: a political nobility that is immune to the people's will. They have created through our campaign and lobbying laws a series of incentives that corrupt the intent of the Constitution.

It's time to make a few changes. Specifically, we need to insist on a sweeping package of reforms for our political system:

- Restrict campaign contributions to $1,000—period. No more "soft money" contributions of up to $100,000 from corporate interests, labor unions, and rich people. No more $8-million extravaganzas where the dinner seating is determined by how much money you gave to the President's campaign. Think of it. This is the presidency of the United States. This is the office George Washington once held. We will no longer allow it to be demeaned and cheapened by pandering to wealthy donors from all over the world.
- Curb political action committees. In 1974 PACs contributed nearly $13 million to congressional candidates. About that time lobbyists noticed that congressmen returned their phone calls if their PAC had given money. In 1990, PACs contributed over $150 million, an eleven-fold jump. Who are we trying to kid here? We know what they're out to buy. It's time for the owners of the country to declare that the United States Congress and the White House are not for sale.
- Give the Federal Election Commission real teeth.

Right now, the President appoints six members. By tradition there are three Republicans and three Democrats. Guess how many tie votes there are. You can also guess at the amount of winking and nodding that goes on around the table. No wonder it's a paper tiger. It must be revamped. Let's have five members appointed at staggered terms. Give it criminal prosecution powers to enforce our election laws.

• Change the way we hold elections. First, shorten the campaign season. Five months is long enough for anyone to make a case. Hold elections on both Saturday and Sunday so working people can go to the polls. Release no information until all polls are closed. Since the airwaves belong to the public, require equal free time for candidates for federal office. Joined with easier voter registration, these measures will improve our elections and stimulate more voters to go to the polls.

• Eliminate the electoral college. There's no reason to filter the people's vote. Why shouldn't we let the people directly choose their President and Vice President? Whoever gets the most votes of the entire country should be the President.

Public Service Is a Public Trust

Reforming our campaign laws is only the beginning. We have to restore the idea that public service is a sacred trust. Being an elected, appointed, or career public servant is a noble calling. Some of our elected and appointed officials see their terms of office as interim steps to high-paying lobbying jobs. We need to make it abundantly clear that anyone who enters the federal government comes to serve, not to cash in.

- Make it a criminal offense for any foreign government or individual or company to attempt to influence American laws or policies by means of direct or indirect campaign contributions. Tighten laws requiring full and prompt disclosure.
- Rewrite the foreign agent registration and lobbying laws to close the loopholes. Today there is not even a clear definition of what lobbying is. For example, if you don't want to be accused of hiring a lobbyist, you hire a law firm to accomplish the same task.
- Forbid any former President, Vice President, cabinet officer, agency director, Federal Reserve governor, commission director, White House staffer, trade negotiator, member of the Senate or House from accepting one penny for any reason from any foreign interest— ever. Anybody who holds one of these high offices does so because the American people gave them their trust. That trust should be honored.
- Forbid anyone who has held any position in the federal government to be a paid lobbyist for any domestic interest for five years after leaving government. Slam the revolving door shut.
- Draft a tough ethics code for private citizens who serve as consultants and advisers to the federal government. The federal government contracts with these private citizens, most of whom used to work for the government, to do the work that federal employees could do. These people usually get paid much more than workers on the federal payroll. Establish stiff criminal penalties for any abuse or fraud.

• Forbid anybody on the payroll of a foreign government or foreign interest from serving in any capacity, volunteer or paid, in a presidential or congressional campaign. Right now, foreign lobbyists play key roles in both the Democratic and Republican campaigns. That is inexcusable.

Clean Up the Executive Branch

At a time when we're asking the American people to make sacrifices for their country, why do we allow our political elites to live like pampered royalty? No wonder the American people have grown disgusted with their government; we need to take severe steps to restore that sacred trust.

• Move immediately to sell off the 111 civilian aircraft maintained for discretionary use by federal government executives. Conduct a case by case review of the remaining 1,100 civilian planes owned by the federal government that are allotted to different legislative and executive agencies. Keep the few that are essential.

• Eliminate the 89th wing of the air force. It exists solely to transport top officials around the country. The Cold War is over. The Vice President doesn't need an air force jet to go play golf. I don't understand how a chief of staff to the President could even consider using a government jet to take him to the dentist.

People might say, "Aren't you being a little hard? These people have giant responsibilities while running huge departments of government. Most corporate executives never run anything so large and complex, and they all have corporate jets."

These people work for *us*. They are our employees. Unless we take steps like this, they will continue to believe we work for them.

We need to capture their hearts and minds. No matter how high their office or how lofty their titles, members of the next administration should fly commercially. They should go out to the airport, get in line, lose their baggage, eat a bad meal, and stay in touch with how normal people live. Then, if there's a recession in this country, it won't take three months for them to figure it out. The person in the seat next to them will let them know in no uncertain terms.

• Have the cabinet members spend most of their time outside Washington anwering tough questions and solving real problems. What good can the Secretary of Education do behind a desk while our schools are falling apart? How can the Secretary of Health and Human Services tackle the massive bureaucratic problems of this system without really understanding the people who encounter them?

• Encourage federal employees to treat citizens as owners. When *any* owner of this country walks into a federal office, that person should be treated with the courtesy and respect that an owner should receive. We need to restore pride in the federal service so that our employees will smile every day at the office and be polite.

• Reduce civil service restrictions and allow more discretion so that federal employees can be more responsive. The word "bureaucrat" conjures up some bloodless, uncaring robot with a rubber stamp. In

28

truth, I've found almost every federal employee I've encountered to be a dedicated, intelligent professional. We need to lift restrictions that keep our employees from doing their best jobs. We need fewer employees and more rewards.

We need to give our officers the tools to do the job. Right now, for example, the Secretary of Housing and Urban Development presides over a department of 13,000 people. By legislative statute he can only hire or fire 105 of them. It's not surprising that public housing is a mess.

• Drastically cut the White House and executive branch staffs. John F. Kennedy had a White House staff of 600. George Bush has 1,850. In 1960, Congress had a total staff of 5,610. Today it has a staff of over 20,000. What do all these people do? From my experience, their main mission is to insulate executive officials and members of Congress from you, the owners. Their secondary mission is to make sure their boss gets reelected. Congress and the executive branch have grown fat, complacent, unwieldy, and unresponsive. The White House and Congress could easily reduce their staffs by 30 percent.

Never forget that staffs accomplish very little. All of the action is in the field.

Look at the Agriculture Department to see how much the bureaucracy in the executive branch has grown. In 1948, farms employed 20 percent of our population, and the Agriculture Department had 67,000 employees. It was considered a huge bureaucracy. Today only 2 percent of our people work on farms, but the Agriculture Department has swollen to 118,000 employees. Instead of creating a new cabinet office every time a special interest group wants more attention, we should overhaul and permanently reduce departments of government so that we can apply our resources where they will do more good for our people. We don't need staffers in Washington to hold a cabinet officer's briefcase. We need hands-on problem solvers out in the field where they will do some good.

Restore Confidence in Congress

Congress needs to take a good, hard look at itself as an institution. It has been through trying times. It has in large measure lost the respect and confidence of the American people. We cannot afford to let this go on. A representative democracy depends on the essential trust the people place in their institutions. We should urge Congress to regain that trust by taking four measures immediately:

• Slash the current $2.8 billion budget that supports Congress, its agencies, gymnasiums, staffs, barber shops, free mail, and all the other perks that have been built up over the years. Cut congressional staffs by 30 percent and other perks by 40 percent. Congress could apply nearly $1 billion toward cutting the deficit. Suddenly the people, the financial markets, our allies, and our competitors would realize that the United States is serious about facing its problems. Congress would rise to new heights of respect in everyone's eyes by becoming more productive.

• Reform the retirement system. Up to 93 members of Congress are eligible for lifetime pension benefits exceeding $2 million apiece. This is *much* higher than their constituents' pensions! The people consider such excesses a breach of trust.

• Reorganize the legislative system. As many as fifteen committees and subcommittees must be involved for any significant piece of legislation to pass the House. Negotiations among all these committees and subcommittees become so complex that loopholes and special favors get enacted with only a handful of people knowing about it. Congress needs to streamline this process so that they and the people can follow the progress, or lack of it, on bills before the House and Senate. Members of Congress should be acutely aware that the people run this country, not the lobbyists in the hallways and offices.

• Turn in excess campaign funds to the Treasury. Some congressmen have racked up campaign war chests which hold many millions of dollars. Every two years, the PACs pour more money in just to stay in their good graces. Clean it up. The owners want that money back.

Restore a Sense of Ownership to Our People

Owners have responsibilities, too. If you have guests in your house, and you allow them to pocket the loose change on the dresser, you have nobody to blame but yourself when you discover they've stolen your television set. The most honest people in the world will be corrupted by a pattern of winking at minor misdemeanors. By the time they get to the television set they've lost all sense of proportion. They've begun to believe that they deserve it and that nobody will mind. If that's the psychology at work with people in your own home, magnify it a million times to understand the problem that festers in Washington.

Again, if you want to know who's to blame for our political system that encourages and rewards people who cash in on public service, look in the mirror.

We have abdicated our responsibilities as owners. Our political system can only be repaired if we take charge of it.

• First, all of us must vote. We need legislation to make voter registration more accessible. How can anyone disagree? We should change the voting time from Tuesday to both Saturday and Sunday.

• Second, we must stay informed. I've suggested we have an interactive "Electronic Town Hall" so that as a nation we can lay out the issues, review the choices, argue over the merits and demerits, and reach a consensus. This has aroused a lot of controversy, but why? Most of us carry on a quiet debate with our leaders every morning while we're reading the newspapers. I remember that FDR's "Fireside Chats" united us as a country and set a national direction. President Reagan used the same medium to explain his ideas. The only difference between the Fireside Chat and the Electronic Town Hall is that the first was one-way, the only radio technology available at the time, and the second is two-way, which we can do today. Instead of passively listening to the radio or watching members of the political elite debate on television, our citizens will be able to engage their representatives and appointed officials in a direct conversation. This may be a conversation our political elites would like to avoid, and I can understand why. That doesn't mean they should be able to avoid it. For our system to work, our elected officials must listen to the owners (us) we, the people.

Eternal vigilance is the price of liberty, and citizen participation is the price of responsible representative democracy. This is what our Founders intended and what we must restore.

Fix the System First

We must repair the political system. If we don't, the actions we take to repair our economic engine will be just another series of temporary fixes. We have to change the incentives if we expect our political leaders to hold the course in setting this country right. Let's tackle this like our grandparents would have. Let's fix it. Then let's keep it fixed. Do it as an act of love for our grandparents and parents who gave us this country, and also for our children and grandchildren. They deserve the very best government we can give them.

CHAPTER THREE

An America that Pays Its Way

For a decade the United States economy has been pulled and tugged from two different directions. Republicans in the White House pushed for lower taxes on the rich in the hope that their increased incomes would *trickle down* to the rest of the nation. Meanwhile, Democrats in Congress pushed for *tax and spend* policies that would take more money out of all our pockets and put it into big government programs. The result is that nothing trickled down, we all got taxed, and government spending skyrocketed. The Federal government's share of our gross national product increased from 19 percent to 25 percent over the past twenty years.

In the 1960s and 1970s we were led to believe government could solve our problems. It couldn't, and it made some problems worse.

In the 1980s we were led to believe the private economy could solve our problems. It couldn't, and it didn't. Some people became richer. A lot more became poorer. Most families just got stuck. The average family purchasing power in 1992 is about where it was in 1976 in real dollars.

Our two parties are locked into their ideologies. The Democratic Party's platform this year admits tax and spend policies don't work. Then it goes right ahead to offer a program of massive government spending (called "investment") which will have to be paid for by higher taxes or even more debt. The Republicans, still clinging to the hope that our economy will right itself on its own, offer no program at all.

We cannot afford to let either party's ideology continue to wreak havoc on our economy.

Our first priority is to balance the budget. The United States government must pay its way. There are only two ways to do it: reduce spending and generate revenues. It's that simple. In your family, when you can't pay the bills, you either get a raise or start cutting back to the necessities. In any business, big or small, it's the same. Government tries to sneak around this principle, either by borrowing money or by printing it. These end runs never work. They always compound the problem because they don't address it.

As a nation, we have to make some hard choices that involve setting our priorities. Elected officials back away from this like a dog backs away from an angry cat. They're worried about getting scratched in the face by some angry special interest. Yet, every American has to make hard choices every day. Do I need a new car? Not really. Can I afford a week at the beach? No. Do the children need new clothes? Yes. Should I pay down my Visa account? I'd better. Can we afford a house? Let's check the interest rates.

These are everyday questions, not life-shattering philosophical decisions. They shouldn't be too hard. Yet, ask an elected official if he wants more money for either Head Start or public television. He'll quickly calculate who gives him what and how it will look on the evening news, then he will answer he wants both. That's an answer we can't afford to receive anymore.

We need to lay out the choices and then give the officials no place to hide. The choices may be painful, but they must be plain and clear. Government is not a candy store in which every group can pick from any jar it wants. This is not free money. It's your money, and more importantly, it's your children's money. Under our present system, our elected representatives can retire to Hawaii when the bad news comes. But where will your children be? What kind of education will your grandchildren receive? Where will their jobs come from?

It is unconscionable not to act now. My own experience with General Motors is a case in point. In the mid-eighties it had plenty of money and time to recreate itself as a company dedicated to excellence. The corporate bureaucracy, however, wouldn't budge. Neither top management nor the board of directors would deal with the real problems. During the past year, GM lost almost $400 million a month. It is now in the process of firing employees, closing plants, permanently downsizing. It wouldn't have happened if its owners, the shareholders, had demanded that the Board look into the future and make the difficult decisions early on.

I started as a salesman for IBM, one of the most successful business enterprises ever. I believed twenty years ago that IBM would grow forever. Today it is a company playing defense, not offense.

Time is not our friend. We must start now to cut the huge budget deficit.

What follows is my proposal of exactly how the budget should be balanced. As the graph on deficits shows, this plan will get rid of the deficit by 1998. Compare the results of this plan to what the deficits are estimated to be if current policies are followed by Congress.

It is not a perfect plan, but it is fair and reasonable. I urge all of you, including the two political parties, to improve upon it.

Cut Discretionary Spending

Require the federal departments to submit budgets that cut 15 percent from their discretionary budgets in two steps. First, cut specific programs that are unnecessary or outdated to save 5 percent. Then, make an across-the-board cut of all remaining departments and programs of another 10 percent. This will save $108 billion over five years. In my business experience the one overriding lesson is that the longer an enterprise is in existence, the larger the unnecessary overhead. It's human nature. Give some people a nice position, and soon they want two assistants instead of one; they want their nameplate in brass; and they think they deserve

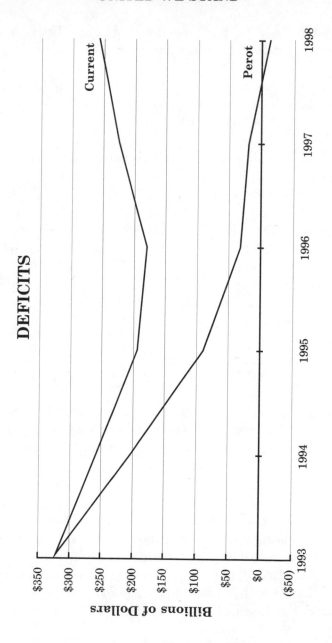

DEFICITS

a private dining room. It is time to adjust our spending to what we can afford.

Let me give you two examples of programs that we don't need:

First, we are spending money on programs that are nice but not necessary. One example is the space station. I'm a supporter of scientific research. However, this is a huge undertaking for a nation with an operating deficit of over $330 billion. We should defer the space station until we have the money to pay for it.

We are spending on programs that have long since outlived their usefulness. The Rural Electrification Administration was set up during the New Deal to provide electrical power to our outlying rural areas where no power company could afford to go. It did its job. The country is now electrified and the program should be phased out.

There are many other candidates for elimination. Every program must be evaluated objectively. We should save only those programs we need for our future.

Enact the Line Item Veto

The last five Presidents have requested it, and 43 governors have it. When budget resolutions come back to the President's desk studded with little rhinestones for special interest groups, he should have the authority to pluck them off. Those rhinestones are stuck on by powerful members of Congress to enhance their reputations back home or to repay the special interests that gave them PAC money. The President is forced, under the present system, to either accept the entire bundle, rhinestones and all, or veto the whole thing. This is bad budget procedure.

Congress ought to have the last say. They would still have the right to override a line item veto with a two-thirds majority.

Enact a Real Deficit Reduction Law

Congress needs a mechanism to keep our fiscal house in order. When we talk about the budget, we're talking about a mirage. Our government mostly operates by a series of continuing resolutions, not by a budget. This system is clumsy, inefficient, and open to abuse by special interests. Congress must manage its own business before it can undertake the people's.

A strong, consistent deficit reduction law is necessary, and I believe it would be welcome in Congress. I believe Congress rejected the proposed balanced budget amendment because they knew it was phony. Why tamper with the Constitution when what we need is for Congress to apply restraint over its own procedures?

Eliminate Special Favors

Thousands of special favors for various groups are in the budget. Space doesn't allow me to name every single one, but I will give some examples:

The inland waterways are costly to patrol and maintain. The private companies that benefit from them ought to pay for their use. Similarly, people who cut timber on public lands should pay full cost for the privilege. In general, we should adopt user fees for many public services that benefit only a portion of the population.

We should eliminate special tax favors, such as those for alcohol-fuel and iron-ore shipping companies.

We should eliminate protective tariffs for such commodities as sugar. Because of what lobbies have gained, we pay increased prices at the grocery store. If lower tariffs hurt small farmers in the short run, we should have programs that reward them for more productive activities.

We should eliminate our entire system of farm subsidies for giant agricultural corporations.

We should cut deductions for business meals and entertainment to 50 percent of the cost. Now 80 percent are deductible. I don't know many working people who take them. I'm a businessman, and I know they are sometimes necessary expenses. I also know I have to eat lunch whether I'm doing business or not.

By cutting various unnecessary subsidies and tax favors, we would save $50 billion over five years.

Cut the Defense Budget to Meet Its Mission

Nothing is more important than the security of our country. In the post–Cold War world, however, our well-being depends less on *military* security than on *economic* security. On the military side, we have the resources, the strategic doctrine, and the hardware in place to confront any serious threat to our interests anywhere in the world. We don't need to be ready to fight World War III tomorrow because World War III is not going to break out tomorrow.

Our military budget is stuffed with relics from the Cold War, such as the B-2 and the Seawolf submarine. We don't need them. What's more, we can't afford them. I propose that they be eliminated.

I have great respect for the men and women who serve our country in the armed forces. I suggest implementing a program to provide a smooth transition for these talented and well-trained people to reenter the job force. They will make a tremendous addition to the productivity of our nation. American companies should avail themselves of this unparalleled opportunity to employ these dedicated people.

Similarly, we need to convert many of our defense industries to new and productive tasks so that the downsizing of our defense is not accompanied by a downturn in jobs. The federal government can play an important role. Many of these companies are among our finest in research and technology. They can be instrumental in restoring our lead in new technologies.

First we need to implement a well-conceived and deliberate plan to restructure the defense budget to match the post–Cold War reality. In doing so, we can save at least an additional $40 billion during the five years over the cuts proposed by President Bush.

Stop Subsidizing the Rich

Under current law the federal government allows homeowners to deduct from their income taxes interest on mortgages up to one million dollars. Why should we subsidize interest on huge, expensive homes? I know people who own two houses: one as their principal residence and another on the beach. Because the mortgages on both total under one million dollars they deduct every penny from their taxes. Why should we subsidize interest on vacation homes?

The average mortgage in the United States is $104,-000. I propose that we limit deductions on interest to mortgages of $250,000 and that we eliminate the special deduction for vacation homes.

Another subsidy for the rich is the exemption from taxes on expensive employer-paid health insurance. These plans support the rich and encourage excessive health costs. They should be taxed as additional income. I propose that all such contributions over $335 for a family and $135 for an individual each month—which is more than most of us get—be taxed.

These two measures alone would save us $72.9 billion over five years.

In addition, we should raise the marginal tax rate on the wealthy from 31 to 33 percent. In 1993, this change would affect individuals who make over $55,550 and joint filers who make over a total of $89,250. Therefore, less than 4 percent of the taxpayers in America will be affected, but we will raise $33 billion in five years. If other reductions proposed here do not provide sufficient revenue, we should be prepared to raise the marginal rate to 35 percent.

Control Entitlement Costs

Our biggest problem is entitlement programs. These include Social Security, government retirement, medicare, and medicaid. They now consume 50 percent of the federal budget. The accompanying chart on entitlement outlays shows how much we spend on them. They are the fastest growing part of our budget, and they are growing at an alarming rate. The combined costs of medicare and medicaid doubled in the last six years. If we don't take action now, we won't have the money to support them.

These programs are the heart of our social services. Millions of people depend on them every day, and they must be secure in the absolute knowledge these programs will continue. The President must act as guardian at the gate to protect these programs against any threat.

The threat I fear the most is that their runaway costs will outstrip the nation's ability to pay for them.

The reason these are called entitlement programs is that they run on automatic. Congress and the White House, influenced by politicians of both parties, have set them up so they never have to confront the political problem of dealing with them. That's why they've grown unchecked. The accompanying graph shows how wildly entitlements have jumped from 1960 to 1991.

They've also grown out of whack. Families with high incomes actually received more entitlement benefits than poor families in 1991, and much more than middle class families.

44

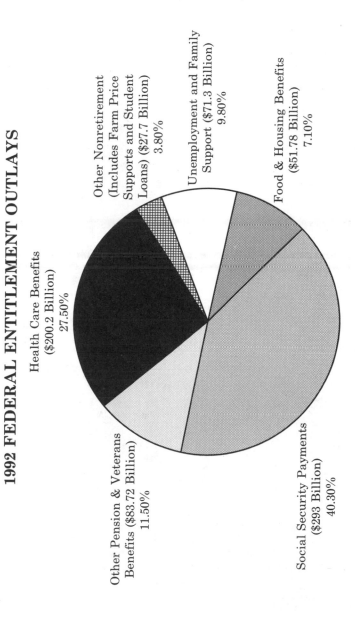

1992 FEDERAL ENTITLEMENT OUTLAYS

Health Care Benefits
($200.2 Billion)
27.50%

Other Nonretirement
(Includes Farm Price
Supports and Student
Loans) ($27.7 Billion)
3.80%

Unemployment and Family
Support ($71.3 Billion)
9.80%

Food & Housing Benefits
($51.78 Billion)
7.10%

Other Pension & Veterans
Benefits ($83.72 Billion)
11.50%

Social Security Payments
($293 Billion)
40.30%

FEDERAL ENTITLEMENT GROWTH

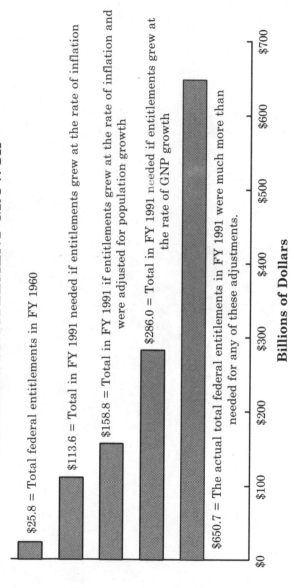

$25.8 = Total federal entitlements in FY 1960

$113.6 = Total in FY 1991 needed if entitlements grew at the rate of inflation

$158.8 = Total in FY 1991 if entitlements grew at the rate of inflation and were adjusted for population growth

$286.0 = Total in FY 1991 needed if entitlements grew at the rate of GNP growth

$650.7 = The actual total federal entitlements in FY 1991 were much more than needed for any of these adjustments.

Billions of Dollars

$0 $100 $200 $300 $400 $500 $600 $700

These programs can be saved, and our fiscal sanity restored, by taking some fairly simple steps.

First, those who can afford it should pay more to support the program. Better-off Americans stop paying medicare taxes on income over $130,000 a year. We should lift that cap.

Second, given the size of the problem, everyone except the poorest among us should share in the changes. Users of the medicare supplemental medical insurance program should pay premiums of 35 percent of program costs, up from 25 percent today. The program was originally designed to be financed at 50 percent by users.

These two steps alone would raise $66 billion over five years.

Our federally funded pension plans will cost us $348 billion this year. These necessary programs can be protected if we manage them with care. First, all retirees who can afford it should pay taxes on their Social Security benefits just as they do on private pension benefits. Now those elderly who make over $25,000 per year as individuals or $32,000 filing jointly pay taxes on 50 percent of their benefits. Taxing an additional 35 percent of the benefits for those who already pay taxes will affect only 18 percent of retirees but will raise $30 billion over five years.

In addition, retirees from federal government service, military and civilian, would have their cost of living *increases* reduced by one-third over the next five years under my proposal. Nobody will receive a penny less than they receive today. In fact, they will continue to receive more every year. Decreasing by a small percentage the increases we make in these payments , would produce $13 billion in savings over five years.

The biggest savings we can achieve in our entitlement programs is through a reform of our entire health care system. I discuss this at greater length in Chapter 5, but my goal is to improve both the quality and delivery of medical services through medicare and medicaid for a savings of over $141 billion over five years.

Increase Tobacco and Gasoline Taxes

We need to increase tobacco taxes. We can raise over $18 billion over five years. Smoking kills more than 400,000 people every year. Some of this money can be used to increase research for cures to related diseases. These diseases are costing us over $20 billion a year in medical costs. At the same time, because of the power of the tobacco lobby and its effect on some key senators and members of the House, we subsidize the growing of tobacco with your money. That doesn't make sense.

Also, I will propose a ten-cent increase in the gasoline tax for each of the next five years. This will raise approximately $158 billion. The basic purpose is to use these funds to create jobs by rebuilding our crumbling national highway system, building high-tech, sensible transportation networks, and building a telecommunications system for the 21st century. Our infrastructure is a fundamental element in world economic competition. The Japanese, for example, plan to invest over six times per capita more than we do in the 1990s. Even Taiwan, about the size of Pennsylvania, intends to spend three times more per capita than we do on its infrastructure in the next decade.

There is another reason to increase the gasoline tax. The United States depends on foreign sources for about 40 percent of its oil. Our long-term national security requires that we reverse this trend. We cannot allow our economy to be held hostage to oil sheiks and petty dictators in one of the most unstable regions of the world. Finally, of course, reducing the consumption of gasoline will curb pollution.

As the graph shows, Americans would pay far less than citizens of other countries for each gallon of gasoline even with this increased tax.

At the same time, I am sensitive to the hardship that this tax proposal may impose on some people such as small farmers and independent truckers. We should allow tax deductions and other adjustments to relieve such hardship

Increase Collections

We charge the IRS with the mission of collecting $1 trillion a year, yet we have been slow to give them the tools to do the job. The IRS is now in the process of upgrading its computer systems. We must recruit the finest engineers and best software people in private industry to review their plans, suggest improvements, and aid them in speeding up the process. Some have estimated that $50 to $100 billion could be saved each year. Surely we can find $10 billion of that over the five years of the plan.

In addition, our lax tax treatment of foreign companies operating in the U.S. costs us at least $21 billion over five years. That must be corrected.

We need to equalize and simplify the tax code. Our current system is like an old inner tube covered with patches. Most of the patches were put there to protect

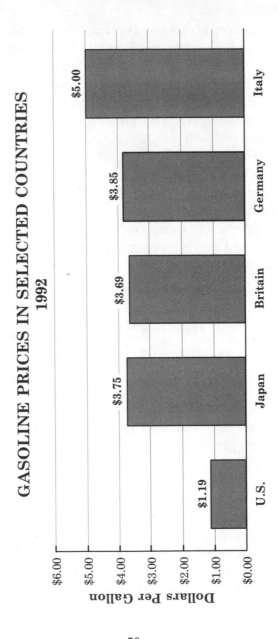

GASOLINE PRICES IN SELECTED COUNTRIES
1992

Dollars Per Gallon

$6.00
$5.00
$4.00
$3.00
$2.00
$1.00
$0.00

U.S. $1.19
Japan $3.75
Britain $3.69
Germany $3.85
Italy $5.00

some special interest. We need a new, simpler system. One, it must be fair for everyone. Two, it should be paperless for most people. Although the new system will not cause tax rates to rise, it will cause overall revenues to rise because it would eliminate many of the gimmicks that lawyers and accountants employ to gain advantages for their clients.

Get Our Allies to Share the Burden

For forty-five years we have defended Japan and Germany. It has been a necessary investment in our own security. Two things have plainly changed: one, the threat of a hostile superpower poised to attack us has vanished. Two, we can't afford it anymore.

Collective security is still a common goal we should continue to pursue. Let's make it truly common. Asia and Europe should pay $100 billion toward their own defense. I fully realize this might, for example, double Germany's and Japan's defense budgets. But look at the graph on military spending. They now pay *much* less for defense than we do. This is a burden they must accept.

All of us have an interest in maintaining an American presence in Europe and in Asia. All of us are aware of the threat terrorist states pose to our people's safety. All of us are aware that the breakup of the Soviet Union could lead to dangerous situations on both its western and eastern borders. As we face an uncertain future in an uncertain world, all I ask is that the Asian and European countries bear their share of the defense burden with us.

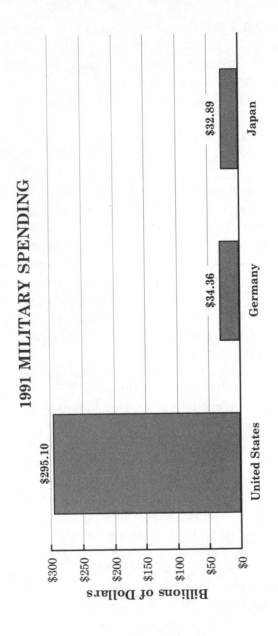

1991 MILITARY SPENDING

Billions of Dollars

$300 $250 $200 $150 $100 $50 $0

$295.10

United States

$34.36

Germany

$32.89

Japan

AN AMERICA THAT PAYS ITS WAY

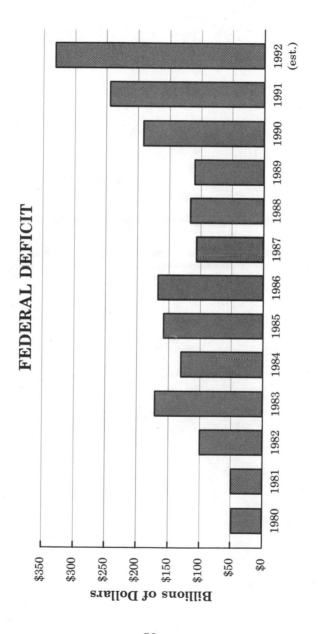

FEDERAL DEFICIT

Billions of Dollars

$0 $50 $100 $150 $200 $250 $300 $350

1980 1981 1982 1983 1984 1985 1986 1987 1988 1989 1990 1991 1992 (est.)

1992 U.S. GOVERNMENT INCOME: $1.1 TRILLION

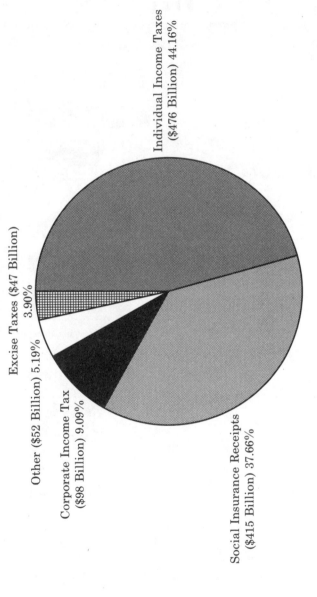

Individual Income Taxes
($476 Billion) 44.16%

Excise Taxes ($47 Billion)
3.90%

Other ($52 Billion) 5.19%

Corporate Income Tax
($98 Billion) 9.09%

Social Insurance Receipts
($415 Billion) 37.66%

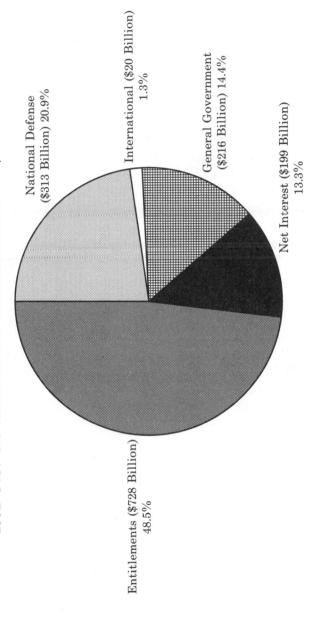

1992 U.S. GOVERNMENT EXPENDITURES: $1.5 TRILLION

National Defense ($313 Billion) 20.9%

International ($20 Billion) 1.3%

General Government ($216 Billion) 14.4%

Net Interest ($199 Billion) 13.3%

Entitlements ($728 Billion) 48.5%

Is It Possible?

Can we repair the damage to our economy, permanently cut the size of government, protect the programs so necessary to our people, and rid our children of this massive load of debt?

Yes.

By taking these steps, we can save $754 billion over five years. In the fifth year we will have a budget surplus of $10 billion.

This $754 billion will not be allowed to fall into the black hole of government. It will not go to special interests. It will not be squandered away on new programs or favorite causes of members of Congress. We will permanently reduce the cost of government. Except for the tax revenues committed to special purposes, it will go to the American people to invest and to save.

Many Americans have lost confidence in our government. You must not walk away. You have the vote. You are the owner. You can study the facts. You can demand that they be changed.

You are the owner. Only you can rebuild America.

Individually you have no voice. Together, we can change the world.

CHAPTER FOUR

An America that Prospers

"**M**ade in the USA" can once again become the world's standard for excellence. The United States can again become the preeminent economic power on earth.

Nothing can stop us, except ourselves.

When the Japanese planes returned to their carriers from bombing Pearl Harbor, the fleet's second-in-command turned to Admiral Yamamoto. "You have won a great victory, sir," he beamed. The Admiral turned away unsmiling, stared out at the horizon, and said, "You don't understand. We have awakened a sleeping giant."

Six months later the American fleet crushed the Japanese in history's first great air-sea battle at Midway Island.

There is nothing to stop us from being the most productive nation on earth. There is nothing to stop us from creating jobs that produce real wealth for our working people. With strong leadership and involved citizens, there is nothing to stop us from creating new industries and technologies that will dazzle the world.

We are up against fine competitors. They know how to work. They know how to finance their industries. They know how to produce excellent products. *They know how to use government to promote their growing economies.*

Like it or not, we live in a tiny world. The international competition is fierce. Every day somebody wins and somebody loses. In business they don't hand out red ribbons when you lose. Instead, they hand out pink slips, close factories, put families on welfare, and shut down entire towns.

America must be put back to work.

The next administration must move immediately to stimulate thousands and perhaps even millions of new small businesses, to target industries of the future where American know-how can take the lead, and to break down the adversarial relationship between business and government that sends jobs overseas.

Create New Jobs

The vast majority of our new jobs won't come from our biggest employers. They will come from our smallest. Americans are by nature an entrepreneurial people. Almost everyone has an idea for a new product, a new service, a new shop, a new kind of delivery system, a new way to make a living and maybe even to make a fortune. We've got to do everything we can to make these dreams a reality.

- *Free up credit.* The deregulation of our banks and savings and loans was poorly thought through and poorly executed. Now we have to repair the damage. Our small businesses are starved for credit. People with good ideas can't get loans. The regulators came to a recent board meeting of a savings and loan to read a message from the administration telling them to start making loans. The board listened with utter bafflement. The day before the same regulators had required them to tighten their capital requirements, which meant they couldn't make any new loans. We need government officials who understand credit and take the lead in restructuring our credit markets to give access to small businesses so they can invest for growth.
- *Stimulate investment.* We can establish incentives through the tax code and in other ways to stimulate the creation of capital pools for small business where the risk is spread out and thereby reduced. Most new businesses are founded on less than a $100,000 investment.
- *No capital gains tax for small business investment.* We should eliminate any tax on gains made for investment in starting small businesses. This is the quickest and surest way to convince investors to take the risk of backing entrepreneurial ventures.
- *Establish mentor programs.* Small businesses fail for two reasons: lack of money and lack of experience. We have a huge resource in our talented retired people. Our retirees are younger and more fit than at any other

time in our history. Let's put them to work. Programs are already in place that demonstrate how effective retired executives can be in mentoring young companies.

Today very talented college graduates can't get jobs. Well-trained and highly disciplined military personnel coming out of the armed services don't have jobs. These people know how to organize. They know how to execute. We need to stimulate the private sector to provide them with mentors, capital, and credit. They will create jobs.

Target Growth Industries

We cannot afford to keep this nation organized to fight the Cold War. We no longer have an enemy. Today we're engaged in a new war for economic survival. We have competitors. We are not threatened with nuclear destruction. We are threatened with economic decline. To a family that just lost its house because it couldn't pay the mortgage, to the single mother who just went on unemployment because she lost her job, to the father who just realized he won't be able to pay his children's tuition for college, this war is real and personal.

We put the entire resources of our nation behind winning the Cold War. We built an interstate highway system because we needed to be able to quickly transport military material and personnel across this continent. We paid for the finest aerodynamic engineering and design because we wanted to dominate the skies. We created NASA because we wanted the quickest and most accurate intelligence on our enemies.

AN AMERICA THAT PROSPERS

Look at the byproducts of the public investments we made in our national security: good transportation routes for commerce, the world's leading aerospace industry, and the satellite communications industry. Where would we be without them?

Where will we be in twenty years if we don't continue to make important public investments?

The Japanese learned from our Pentagon, applied the lesson to business, and proceeded to beat us at our own game. The Japanese ministry of international trade and industry targets industries of the future ten years in advance and then applies prudent incentives to the marketplace to make sure those industries are nurtured and grow. Don't tell me that the Japanese are different: homogeneous, regimented, willing to follow orders. We've been doing the same thing they're doing for forty years but only in defense policy.

Some academics say this is a violation of the free market. Don't they realize that the biogenetics industry is the result of our federally funded research universities and the National Institutes of Health?

I am an advocate of fair, free trade. To keep the free market dynamic and our nation competitive, new industries sometimes need to be fertilized and incubated. If our competitors are looking ten years ahead, we must look fifteen years ahead and beat them.

Instead of continuing to lose whole industries, we must fight to be competitive in every arena of the future. Take a look at your VCR, or your television, or even your telephone. They weren't manufactured here. They may have American names on them, but they were made overseas. We have allowed entire industries to vanish. Our loss is another nation's gain.

We can be winners. We can target and stimulate new industries, applications, and inventions that have not even been conceived of yet. We can nurture them, and we can back them against competition. We can put all our muscle behind industries that produce jobs and a higher standard of living for all Americans.

Put Government on the Side of Jobs and Growth

We have an adversarial relationship between goverment and business. This has got to stop. We need to put government on the side of investment, new industries, and better jobs.

One example of government getting in the way is the Sherman Anti-Trust Act. It was passed in 1890 when we were concerned that our large companies were getting so big they would dominate the market.

Over a hundred years later, isn't it time to face up to the fact that the world has changed? We're no longer competing against each other. We're competing against other countries. Don't worry about our businesses getting too big; worry about our businesses getting too small. Nobody needs to be frightened about General Motors taking over the automotive industry. We've got to be concerned about General Motors *succeeding* in the automotive industry. It's time for Congress to wake up to the new realities and stop clinging to the ideas of the past. We urgently need substantial revision of laws that impede our ability to compete.

We can't have employees without employers. We need to relieve the immense burden of paperwork we have placed on small businesses. Anybody with under one hundred employees should only have to fill out a one-page form once a year. That's for Social Security, unemployment compensation, health insurance, safety regulations, and compliance with civil rights legislation. We've turned our small businessmen into bureaucrats. We have more than enough bureaucrats already. We must free our small business people to improve their products, to perfect their services, and to be successful so that they can grow and hire more people.

We can depend on the ingenuity and hard work of our people. Americans know how to get the job done. Government's role should be to support business: creating jobs and creating taxpayers.

Once we make these changes, nothing can hold America back from becoming the leading economic superpower on earth.

Encourage Savings

I talk to people in all walks of life. I sense this current recession has had one good effect. "Let the good times roll" will definitely not replace "In God We Trust" as our national slogan. For a while I was worried.

Nobody believes any longer that their home equity values will rise indefinitely, giving them a tidy nest egg for retirement. In fact, in this recession many home values have declined. Many people have seen their down payments eaten away. Nobody believes that their paychecks will increase ahead of inflation every year. Most feel fortunate to have a paycheck at all. Everyone knows someone who is unemployed. Nobody in the baby boom generation that I've met believes any longer that he or she will be able to count on Social Security being solvent twenty-five or thirty years from now when it's time for their retirement. Many believe they will have to provide for themselves.

This is not happy news, but we can turn it to good use. We can declare as a people that our national spending spree is over. Now we can redirect our energy to building our savings.

We need to replenish our national savings pool so that we have capital to invest. We're saving at a rate of 4 percent compared to the Japanese at 18 percent and the Germans at 10 percent. This is not just dry economic theory. Capital is the very lifeblood of the capitalist system. Capitalism simply can't operate without capital. Our economic engine needs capital, and it needs it now.

We need it for two good reasons.

First, our companies now pay a higher cost for money than companies in Japan and Germany. It's tough to compete when your interest payments are higher than your competitors. He can put that extra money into the product—you can't. By increasing our savings, we reduce the cost of investment.

Second, we are borrowing foreign money. Foreign money kept us afloat during the 1980s. That money can leave just as easily as it came. Look at Germany as a case in point. The absorption of East Germany into West Germany's economic bloodstream will cost billions. Germany's excess cash is no longer available to invest in America.

We need to take steps to reinstill the ethic of saving among the American people. I sense the people are ready for it. When this recession ends, I don't believe we'll go back to spending every nickel we earn.

We need to press immediately for pro-savings incentives on all fronts. This problem has been studied and restudied. There are hundreds of good ideas for increasing individual retirement accounts, creating college tuition funds and home equity pools, allowing tax-free personal savings accounts, and offering other solutions to the problem of enlarging our capital base. It is not the world's most difficult task to sift through these ideas, calculate the benefits versus the costs, open up the results to a national debate, and then enact a package of actions to reverse the present trend.

We should do more than that. The Secretary of Education should create a program whereby our children can participate in this great national endeavor. We need to reinstill these values in our culture. Children in America contributed to the Liberty Bonds during World War II. Our children today need to know how important savings are. Our goal should be to ingrain in the next generation the lesson that was temporarily lost in the present one.

Once again, we cannot afford four more years of talk and buck passing. The committees have already met. The studies have already been done. Meanwhile, we're losing industries and jobs by the day.

The American people are ready to act. They need a Congress and a President willing to lead.

Encourage Private Investment

We're not investing in our future. From 1980 to 1989 Japan had an investment rate of 16 percent of gross domestic product. Ours was 4.5 percent. Who is going to win the race?

I grew up in a farming community. Time and time again we were told stories about the farmer so down on his luck that he had to eat his seed corn instead of planting it. Today our companies are eating their seed corn. They ought to be planting it. We can change the incentives to make them want to plant instead of consume.

Once again, there's no reason to sit on our hands and stare at the ceiling. The policies have already been proposed that can reverse our slide and get the economy moving for the long term.

• *Investment tax credits.* We can stimulate growth by providing tax credits to companies that buy productive equipment and machinery.

• *Research and development tax credits.* We need to encourage our companies to put their money into new improvements, new products, and new lines of products.

• *Tax breaks for long-term capital gains.* My Republican friends are wrong to think this is the magic cure-all for what ails us. My Democratic friends are wrong to think this is just a present to the rich. If we want our corporate executives to think long-term, we have to make their investors think long-term. If shareholders aren't squawking for a short-term gain, the company can concentrate on improving its product so it can survive, compete, and grow. We need a stair-stepped capital gains tax, decreasing each year over five years, on shares purchased from public companies with the money going into the treasury to build the company.

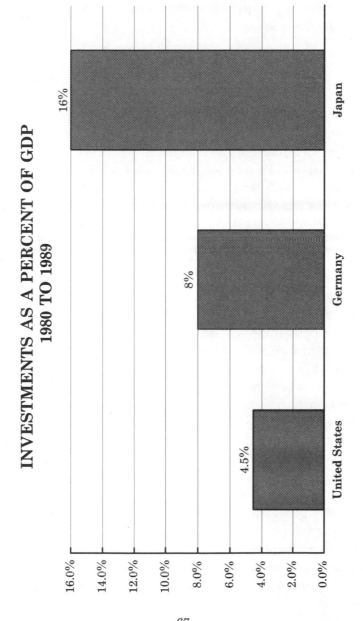

INVESTMENTS AS A PERCENT OF GDP
1980 TO 1989

This would provide the proper incentives to industry and to the market.

Encourage Environmental Protection

This planet is our home. If we destroy the planet, we've destroyed our home.

America has always valued its wealth of natural resources, next to its people, as its most important asset. When we pollute our air and contaminate our water, waste our energy resources, and destroy our wilderness and wildlife, we squander our national wealth.

When we think about how to use our natural resources, we have to think ahead one hundred years, not just two, five or ten years. We can hand over to our children the world's most dynamic economy and the planet's most beautiful environment.

The principles that should guide us will accomplish protection for our environment while stimulating the growth of our economy.

• Conservation makes basic economic sense. Pollution equals waste. A competitive economy depends on a clean environment. Preventing pollution before it happens is cheaper than cleaning it up afterwards. Recycling and conservation are morally and economically sound policies.

• We should support business strategies for sustainable economic development and assist local communities in making the transition away from dying industries.

• Businesses which depend upon the purchase of

publicly owned resources at below-market prices offer the illusion of prosperity, not the reality. Stop subsidizing inefficient, environmentally destructive activities in the mining and timber industries that promote private gain at public expense.

• Overregulation only fouls things up. Our mission is to clean things up. We spend over $100 billion a year to comply with environmental regulations. We should support incentives over regulations to achieve environmental goals. Give people and businesses an incentive to do things the right way in the first place, and they will.

• We need to take the lead in defining the future of global economic development. It is in our best interests to help countries that seek to stabilize their population growth to decrease poverty.

• American companies should be at the forefront of emerging global markets for environmental technology. In 1980, more than 60 percent of the pollution-control equipment used in the United States was domestically produced. In 1990, the figure was less than 35 percent.

• We should invest in research. On too many environmental questions we don't even have agreement about the scientific facts. We can't operate in the dark. We certainly can't afford to create solutions to problems that may not exist. We need to get the facts straight. We don't need to create false choices. We can't afford a debate that doesn't need to take place.

A strong, considered environmental strategy based on these principles can create growth and jobs, not retard them.

Create a Long-Term Energy Policy

A fundamental part of our approach to the environment is a consistent, long-term energy policy. We recently fought a war that cost precious human lives. It might have been avoided if we were not so dependent on foreign oil. We have ignored our wasteful use of energy sources and the related foreign dependency for far too long. Like so many of our problems, our energy problems call for leadership with an eye to the future.

Let's start with cutting down on imports. We import 40 percent of our energy requirements. One-third of our imports come from Persian Gulf countries and other members of OPEC. We should increase motor fuel taxes which will help reduce this dependency and give us money to create jobs.

We can do more. We need a national policy that conserves fuel through education, research, regulations, and market incentives.

At the same time, we should strive for better balance in the use of the various energy resources available to us, including natural gas, nuclear power, and coal. We should reexamine the heavy regulation of the natural gas industry. It is likely that nuclear power will be a major source of the world's energy in the next century. We should take the lead in developing a safe standard modular reactor and expand our research and education regarding waste disposal.

Coal is our largest single domestic source of energy, and we have more than a two-hundred-year supply at current consumption levels. We should increase research and development efforts to obtain clean-coal technologies. They will be of value to us and to other countries. As good global citizens we should lead the way in finding ways for other countries to grow while preserving the environment.

Finally, there are many alternative, renewable energy sources: solar, hydroelectric, wind, biomass, and geothermal. In most cases the cost of them is now too high to allow much use. That may not always be true. Unfortunately, the government has wasted a good deal of money promoting these sources unrealistically in expensive programs like the synthetic fuels corporation. Nevertheless, we should continue to encourage the future low-cost production of these sources with modest research and development programs.

With all of these efforts we will have a stronger, more productive America.

"Action This Day!"

At England's darkest hour, Winston Churchill rallied his people with stirring words, and he offered much more than just the words. He gave them leadership, decisiveness, and a sense of urgency. On memo after memo now preserved in the archives from the war years, are Churchill's scribbled words "Action this day!"

Churchill successfully instilled in his commanders and ministers the idea that when survival is at stake, any action worth taking is worth taking *now*.

We need this same lesson in our country. We need it instilled in our government, in the Congress, in our industries, and among our people. Stop bickering. Stop blaming each other. Stop posturing for partisan advantage. Stop dodging the hard decisions.

There is work to do.

CHAPTER FIVE

An America that Works

The American dream.

Those three short, simple words encompass the hopes and aspirations of all the peoples on earth. The words are not only short and simple. They are also fragile.

A dream denied can shrivel and die like a raisin in the sun. The President and Congress don't need to look very far to see that the American dream has deteriorated for many people. They only need to look out their windows in Washington, D.C. Here is our nation's capital, with its monuments and parks, its statues and museums. It should represent everything that we are as a people. Instead it represents neglect, incompetence, and shame.

Washington is the murder capital of the nation. By the time its children reach the fifth and sixth grades, 31 percent of them have witnessed a shooting, 43 percent have witnessed a mugging, 67 percent have witnessed a drug deal, and 75 percent have witnessed an arrest. These are fifth- and sixth-graders!

Have we lost our sense of decency? Have we lost our ability to be outraged? Have we given up on the children of our cities?

After all, we created the quagmire we now expect these children to grow up in. We need to face the fact that 72 percent of black children born between 1967 and 1969 have been dependent on welfare for some portion of their young lives. A young male in Bangladesh has a better chance of reaching age 55 than a young male in Harlem.

Go to London, Paris, or Rome. These cities have existed for centuries upon centuries. They are bustling and alive, clean and well-maintained. They, too, have their share of the urban poor. Now revisit the cities we know so well: New York, Philadelphia, Detroit, Los Angeles, or most of our other major cities. These are relatively new, but parts of them are dirty, rundown, littered with abandoned buildings, and ravaged with drugs, crime, and violence.

In my church on the Sunday nearest the Fourth of July we sing "America the Beautiful." Every year I am struck by that one verse: "Her alabaster cities gleam, undimmed by human tears."

Why shouldn't our cities gleam?

Why shouldn't our children be untouched by human tears?

I believe in the American dream. I've experienced it.

I know it not as some faraway ideal but as a living, breathing reality. It exists. It is real. It can happen. It takes work and faith and perseverance and caring. It can never be a gift bestowed by government.

The federal government has tried program after program, and our cities have gotten worse. Instead of figuring out how to develop a solution that works, we assumed that simply spending money would make the problems go away.

For example, we spent billions on urban renewal and model cities programs, but our cities weren't renewed and they're certainly not models.

Neglect doesn't work either.

I believe that most of our people want to share in the American dream. We must put a ladder down to reach them so they can climb out of the mire we've put them in. After so many years it's not surprising if people don't know what a ladder looks like or where it leads. We should reach out to give them a lift to the first rung. We should reawaken in them the dream of what they can achieve if they try to make it up that ladder one step at a time. After that, the climbing is up to them. Soon it will be their turn to reach down and lend a hand. That's the way America is supposed to work.

Reform Education

Failing schools and shoddy performance are undermining our nation's ability to compete and our children's expectations for the future.

If this were only a problem in our inner cities, we could concentrate our attention there. It's not. Even our richest suburban schools and our private schools are failing to produce results that measure up on a global scale. The top 5 percent of American students are matched by the top 50 percent of Japanese students. In a recent math competition, the top 1 percent of American students scored the lowest of the top 1 percent of *any other participating nation.* Bankrupt, exhausted, and struggling, Russia has five million young people studying calculus. The United States has only 500,000. Russia may be bankrupt, but it's planting seeds for the future. When harvest time comes, it will reap the benefit.

We lead the world in only one educational category. We spend more per public school student than any other nation.

I've been personally involved in education for years. I know the territory. In 1983, the governor of Texas asked me to head a committee to overhaul the Texas public school system to improve results. Against fierce opposition from entrenched interests, we were able to make considerable headway. I know it can be done.

From the perspective of those years spent on the front lines, I see the major causes of our educational failure to be these:

- We don't have good preschool training.
- Parents aren't thought of as consumers.
- Schools are bogged down by bureaucracy.
- We don't have national standards. We don't hold local schools accountable for their product.
- We don't reward students and teachers for success.
- We haven't made learning the first priority.
- Our schools aren't organized to meet society's needs.

AN AMERICA THAT WORKS

Don't tell me that money is at the root of the problem because it isn't. We spend billions a year on education. More money poured into the same system will only produce the same results.

We can't expect overnight success. We can start with steps that will turn into strides if we pursue excellence with dedication and hard work.

Today there are programs that have proven successful in regions all over the country. There are new pilot programs just starting up. Washington's role should be to establish the means of measuring results and to encourage the spread of successful programs throughout the country. Washington should show local districts how to reallocate tax money away from things that don't work to things that do. The President must use his "bully pulpit" to press again and again for change. Here are the specific steps I recommend:

1. Establish comprehensive preschool programs. Countless studies have proven that $1 spent on preschool programs will save at least $5 down the line. Thousands of children enter first grade without the necessary learning and social skills needed to succeed. I've seen firsthand how early intervention and development centers can change children from even our most bleak and blighted neighborhoods. I've seen a little four-year-old girl sitting on the wooden steps of a tiny house in a poor area playing the violin with the whole neighborhood gathered around, filled with admiration and pride. She went to a special school. It changed her life. The logo of that school was a thumbprint. The message of that thumbprint, taught to those children every day, is that each person is unique and special, that every person has talents, that if you believe you are somebody you will become somebody. Our children need more than a "head start." Our children need and deserve a "running start."

2. Spend Federal dollars to spread programs that work. The Department of Education currently spends $148 million on "Research, Statistics and Assessment." Most of these studies end up in the files. We don't need more studies. In the small towns and local school districts across America, there are many success stories. We should reallocate the research money to spread the word and to encourage implementation of these successful programs. Let's stop trying to re-invent the wheel.

3. Empower parents. Our system is upside down. The producers—educators, experts, administrators, bureaucrats—have all the power. The customers—parents—have very little power. Let's turn the system rightside up. The producers are better organized, as I know from my own experience. Successful producers listen to their customers. We should start by giving middle class and poor parents the same option that wealthy parents have: choice. We should encourage all school districts to allow parents to choose which school within that district their child will attend. This move alone will put pressure on districts to provide equitable choices, with ready access to all. We should also act to remove any federal obstacles to states allowing choice among public, private, and parochial schools. We won't know if this will work until several states try it on a pilot basis. The time to debate is after the results are in. Washington doesn't have the answers. That's been proved beyond debate. Parents may not have the answers, but they are as close to the problem as anyone will ever get. Nobody else has more reason to care. They should be empowered as consumers to achieve excellence for their children.

4. Restore local autonomy with accountability. Our federal government, our states, and even larger urban school districts hamstring our local schools with bureaucratic orders from on high. Our most successful schools hold one thing in common. They have a determined principal who is an academic leader and who takes pride in the achievements of the students. We can neither bind our principals with regulations nor allow incompetent principals to stay on the job.

5. Establish national standards and measure results. We'll never fix this system until parents, as consumers, can plainly see how schools measure up against one another and against the world competition. This information is practically impossible to obtain today. Parents should be able to know how their elementary school performs against the nation's and the world's. Employers need to know how their local school districts perform against others in their state. Principals and teachers need to see where they are succeeding and where they need to concentrate their resources for improvement. Right now we have a $185-billion enterprise operating essentially in the dark. We shouldn't be surprised that it doesn't work. We need to haul it out into the light of day, measure results, student by student, in a thorough, fair way and publish the results school by school for everyone to see.

6. *Make learning the first priority*. When I first studied the Texas educational system, I was surprised to discover how little time in each school day is actually devoted to learning. Junior high and high school students do not need babysitters. They do not go to school to play. These are young adults, and they go to school to learn. We all want our children to be well-rounded and sociable and involved in activities. However, the public is paying for first things first, and the first thing it is paying for is education. Extracurricular activities should take place at the end of a full day of learning. Participation should be allowed only for those students who have demonstrated their willingness to accomplish their academic goals.

7. *Treat teachers as respected professionals*. Good teachers are the heart of our drive for excellence. They should be rewarded with better pay and with community recognition. Their professionalism should be underscored by holding them to standards as rigorous as their counterparts in law or medicine. We should also broaden the available pool of excellent teachers by reexamining the certification process that often acts more as an obstacle to excellence than as a standard of excellence. College professors, business and legal professionals, and military professionals should be encouraged to teach. We have thousands of non-commissioned and commissioned officers who will reenter the civilian job market as the defense budget decreases. These are experts in the single most successful educational enterprise on earth—the United States military. We should put them to work where we need them the most, in our inner city schools.

8. Make better use of school buildings. We have a vast infrastructure that too often goes unused during part of the day and part of the year. We could use these buildings before and after hours for day-care, routine medical clinics, adult literacy teaching, and other purposes. School districts should be encouraged to stretch their school year and keep the buildings in use. We should draw adults into the learning center of the community's children and try to cultivate shared values by bringing people together.

Right now our federal government continues blindly down the path we put it on a generation ago. That path leads nowhere. We need to change direction. We need to be more concerned with outcomes and results than with maintaining a status quo that has clearly failed. This is the first rung on the ladder to the American dream, and we need to plant each child's foot firmly in place to begin the climb.

Improve Life in Our Inner Cities

Our cities cannot be allowed to die. They are the sinew and muscle of our industrial base. They are filled with people who could add to the productive wealth of our nation.

The key issue in our cities is jobs. A robust and expanding national economy could do more to improve the well-being of our cities than all the handouts ever conceived of. By expanding the economy and by focusing on job creation in our cities, we can turn tax-users into tax-payers. This would build dignity and self-esteem, save the rest of us money, and increase our overall economic strength.

Many of the past programs to aid the cities have fallen victim to the pork-barrel mentality. For example, the original model cities program was meant for only ten to fifteen of our urban centers. By the time it got through Congress it was spread across 150 and diluted to the point of uselessness. The recent bill resulting from the Los Angeles riots found itself held hostage until rural areas received a portion of the money for their own development. The Congressional leadership should show some by keeping Congress focused on attacking our problems, not on trying to make everyone happy.

The way to change our cities is to change the incentives. When the proper incentives are in place, the people themselves take matters into their own hands.

That's why I strongly support *enterprise zones,* with demonstrable, real-world incentives to induce companies to create jobs in our inner cities. The recent package passed by Congress is a watered-down version of what we really need. Congress seems to be afraid that somewhere, somehow, somebody will make money. A strong enterprise-zone package won't encourage big businesses to evade taxes by moving into depressed areas. Big businesses would never take the risk. The right package will encourage the people themselves in those areas to start their own businesses. That's where the jobs will come from.

We have millions of people struggling to get off welfare. We need *income incentives* to enable people who work, even minimally, to see immediate positive results in their monthly income. Right now we punish people who take on jobs or try to save. That's wrong.

We need to restore pride and a *sense of community*. The experimental programs already in place to allow residents in public housing to buy the homes they live in have worked, but once again the incentives aren't there to make them work as well as they could. The new owners don't even have the right to sell their newly fixed-up homes to any seller. They have to sell it back to the government. Sometimes you wonder if the people who write these laws know anything about human nature. We ought to want to motivate people to assume the pride of ownership that will make these communities function again.

Most of our federal employees today are focused on rules and regulations. What good are the rules if the results are what we've seen so far? Throw out all but the most essential rules. Give the elected leadership in our cities and states the tools to do the job, and use the federal government to instigate, prod, and encourage good results throughout the nation.

Reduce Crime and Drug Use

We've been fighting phony wars on crime and drugs. If this were a real war, the enemy could comfortably declare victory. Between 1981 and 1990, the violent crime rate increased 23 percent, the forcible rape rate increased 14 percent, and the aggravated assault rate outpaced all other crimes, rising an astonishing 46 percent. This was during a Republican administration. Republicans like to think of themselves as being tough on crime. If this is tough, I'd hate to see soft. Meanwhile, the Democrats don't have any new ideas either. Maybe it's too unpleasant for them.

In 1990, one murder was committed in the United States every 22 minutes, an all-time high.

Crime is often linked with drugs. More than half the people arrested in our major cities tested positive for one or more illicit drugs.

In 1991, more than one million Americans used crack cocaine or heroin for the first time.

The result? Our people are afraid to go out at night in their own neighborhoods. We're not talking about traveling across town. We're talking about walking the dog. Millions of innocent people have wrongfully been put in jail. They've had to put bars on their windows, multiple locks on their doors, and security alarms everywhere. They've had to turn their houses into prisons while criminals rule the streets.

Crime and drugs cost our country millions of dollars in lost productivity, larger prisons, clogged courts, overworked law enforcement, strained medical and health facilities and personnel, and the terrible social costs of destroyed families and individuals.

We watch on television the awful images of a place like Sarajevo, and our hearts go out to those people. Many of our own cities and towns are mini-Sarajevos every night of the week. We cannot offer hope and succor to the rest of the world if we cannot bring hope and relief to our own crime-ridden streets.

Drugs are the source of many of our rising crime statistics. The drug problem at its core is a reflection of our social decay, resulting from the dissolution of the family structure, lack of economic opportunity, and the decline of individual responsibility. We can't restore virtue by the snap of the fingers. That's no reason not to assert strongly the basic moral precepts by which any decent society lives and by which healthy men and women are raised.

As this message is repeated, especially in our schools, programs must be put in place to help drug addicts escape from the pit they've dug for themselves. Specifically, treatment must be available so that when an addict is ready to confront his or her affliction, help is ready at that moment. Right now more than five million Americans are awaiting drug treatment, including 400,000 teenagers and 100,000 pregnant women. We can only handle 32 percent of the load. The rest are left to fall even deeper into the pit.

Almost 80 percent of prisoners released from state facilities end up back in prison. Our prisons are so overloaded that the majority who commit major crimes serve only one-third of their sentences. This is a terrible fact. One thing that might help is to require mandatory drug testing and counseling for prisoners, parolees and probationers, with automatic penalties for those who fail to stay off drugs.

While lowering demand, we also have to reduce supply. Having 19 different federal agencies and over 40 different programs only leads to duplication of effort, turf battles, and bureaucratic paralysis. To be effective, the federal Drug Czar should have administrative and budgetary responsibility for all our drug control programs, including the coordination of our efforts with other governments.

We've allowed drug and crime syndicates to lure many of our young people into selling drugs. The money's good, but the life expectancy isn't. We need to disrupt the marketing chain and salvage these young people.

We should take these steps:

- Apply all appropriate statutes to prosecute gangs and ask the nation's prosecutors and U.S. attorneys what further legal tools they need.
- Mandate life sentences without parole to persons convicted of three violent crimes, no matter at what age those crimes were committed.
- Make literacy and a marketable skill a precondition for release from prison for criminals convicted of violent crime.
- Make federal facilities, especially former military bases, available to states to establish rehabilitation centers for youths convicted on drug or violent crime charges.
- Try joint public/private experiments in diverting gang members from criminal enterprises to legal profit-making enterprises.

The primary responsibility for law enforcement rests with our state and local governments. So far they have borne the brunt of a losing battle. The federal government can provide active leadership, establish a national strategy, act as the coordinating arm for local governments, and provide financial assistance to help communities plagued by drugs and violence.

We have to face the facts. We are 5 percent of the world's population, and we consume about 50 percent of the world's drugs. We cannot survive if that one statistic holds up much longer. If the measures I've recommended above don't work, let's try new ones. If those don't work, try new ones. Admit mistakes, own up to failure. The American people are tired of a government that tries to hide the facts and paint a rosy picture. We know how tough this plague is to eradicate. We want a government that confronts it day after day, that spells out its failures, and that opens its successes to public debate. That's the only way we'll ever reach the day when a President can stand before the people and honestly say, "We've found the solutions. We're putting them to work right now."

Make Our Health Care the Best in the World

We spend more than anybody else in the world on health care, as the accompanying graph shows. We have 37 million people who aren't covered at all. We rank 15th in life expectancy and 22nd in infant mortality. We're paying top dollar for a front-row box seat, and we're not even getting a bad show from the bleachers.

That's the bad news. The good news is with the money we're spending now we can have the finest, most modern, and most comprehensive health care in the world.

We've been talking about health-care reform since Truman was President. The reason we're talking about it now is because of the ballooning costs. Health-care costs have grown at twice our economic growth rate. They are the fastest growing part of the federal budget except for interest payments on the deficit. Our companies are forced to divert money from jobs, higher wages, and research and development because of sky-

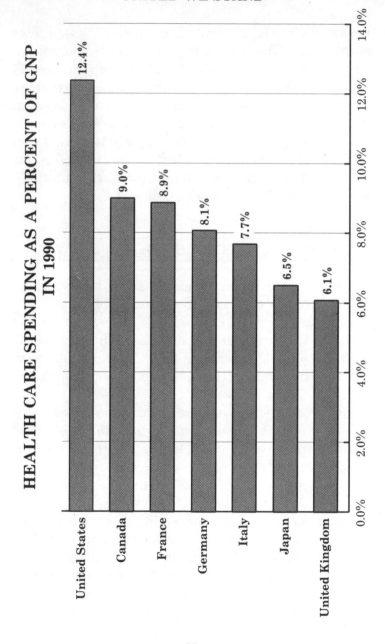

HEALTH CARE SPENDING AS A PERCENT OF GNP IN 1990

United States — 12.4%
Canada — 9.0%
France — 8.9%
Germany — 8.1%
Italy — 7.7%
Japan — 6.5%
United Kingdom — 6.1%

rocketing health and insurance costs.

The need to act has been given a new and terrible urgency by the deadly AIDS epidemic that has already taken such a tragic toll. This plague must be attacked at every level: education, prevention, and accelerated research.

The problem with our health-care system is that it was jerryrigged over many years with a patchwork of different objectives, conflicting demands, colliding interests, and confused incentives. It's not that the programs are bad in themselves. Some, like medicare and medicaid, have done an enormous amount of good. The problem is structural. Health care needs to be reformed.

The political arena is the last place to expect a rational system to be developed. The political system, after all, is ingeniously constructed to allow different groups to push their own interests in the hope that the compromises that result will benefit the whole nation. That has worked fine in some areas. It hasn't worked in reforming a public/private relationship as loaded with pitfalls and potential profit as our health-care system.

I suggest that we should adopt both short-term and long-term strategies. In the short term, a cost containment and prevention program should be developed immediately. Various health-care experts and representatives of affected groups should have a series of work sessions with government officials. A plan should be put into effect as quickly as possible.

In the longer term, comprehensive national health-care reform based on a public-private partnership should involve the following:

- Establishing a national health board as an independent federal agency to oversee cost containment and comprehensive health-care reform efforts
- Setting a national health policy
- Encouraging problem solving by everyone involved
- Reaching a consensus on a set of principles for reform
- Determining a basic benefit package for universal coverage and appropriate tax treatment of health benefits
- Asking states to submit comprehensive health-care reform proposals that meet agreed-upon principles and cost-containment targets
- Changing federal rules to allow states the necessary flexibility to conduct pilot programs.

One important thing should be kept in mind. Preventive action works. "An ounce of prevention is worth a pound of cure." One dollar spent on prenatal care saves more than three dollars of special care for the newborn. One dollar of inexpensive immunizations saves ten dollars of health care and other costs.

It is only a failure of leadership that has kept us from solving this problem. As the problems and dollars mount and our national leaders do nothing, we begin to give in to the notion that nothing can be done. That's baloney. Our health care and medical professionals are the best in the world.

We have the talent. We have the money. We probably even have most of the answers. There are several good plans on paper. We lack leadership. Again, we need "Action this day."

Keep Our Families Strong and Working

The family is the fundamental unit of society. We have to recognize the changes that have occurred in the American family if we are to deal effectively with many of the problems that confront us. We can't just bury our heads in the sand, call ourselves "pro-family," and then pretend that women and families have the same needs they did twenty or thirty years ago. More women are in the workforce today than ever before. Many of these women are mothers. Over half these mothers return to the workplace before their child's first birthday.

One of the keys to preservation of the family unit is job security. If we strengthen our economy, we lessen the pressures of unemployment and low incomes that so often tear families apart. Another key is changing our welfare structure to encourage families to stay together.

When families are torn apart, we must insist that both parents continue to meet their responsibilities to the children. Many children are on public assistance because a parent has refused to pay child support. Congress should pass legislation to make it a felony to cross state lines for the purpose of evading court-ordered child support. We should change the tax code to require parents to report their child-support obligations on their tax-withholding forms. We should also keep a national database on deadbeat parents so they can be tracked and made to pay what they owe to their children.

A Ladder Everyone Can Climb

The whole world thinks of us as the land of opportunity, and we are. However, millions of people are cut off from the blessings this land can provide.

These rungs—better education, revival of our cities, crime control, improved health care, and support for families—can be put firmly in place so that even the most disadvantaged of our people can climb to heights that they can only dream about today. We want to encourage their dreams, but dreams alone are not enough.

No one can ever tell me that the ladders don't matter. No one can tell me we have to give up on generations of our young.

If we have to build those ladders with our own hands, the ladders must be built and put in place.

CHAPTER SIX

An America that Heals

The two most difficult divisions we face as a people are over abortion and race. These divisions are so deep and so ingrained that they require more than a paragraph in this book or more than a soundbite on the evening news. I don't expect to change any minds or win any hearts; I do ask that you read and reflect.

A National Compromise on Abortion

My personal position on abortion is well-known, but I will restate it just to make sure there's no confusion:

- I support a woman's right to have an abortion. It is the woman's choice.

- I support encouragement of adoption as an alternative to abortion.
- I support federal funding of reproductive counseling and education that can help prevent unwanted pregnancies so that fewer women will have to face this difficult decision.
- I support federal funding of abortions for poor women. Since these women have already made the decision, for public health reasons we should ensure that the procedure is done safely.

I believe it is time for Congress to codify these positions into law.

We're thinking, reasoning human beings. Each human life is a precious gift. We should not create a human life unless we're willing to take responsibility for it. It is irresponsible for two people to create a human life they don't want. For democracy to work, for this nation to be whole, every single one of us has to take responsibility for his or her actions.

This is the deepest moral question of our times precisely because it *is* about human life. It is time for moral leadership to heal the rift, to set a new standard of personal responsibility, and to turn both sides toward the enormous task of protecting and nurturing our children.

A National Commitment on Race

"A house divided against itself cannot stand." Many people know Abraham Lincoln said that just before the Civil War. Fewer people recall that he was quoting scripture. What a timeless message and simple truth.

We are divided by racial strife. We're a divided team in worldwide competition against united teams.

We must reunite. I break this down into three approaches. First, we ought to love one another. That takes care of most of us. Second, for those who can't quite lift themselves up to that level, we have to get along with one another so we can team up and win. Third, for the hard-core haters, we're stuck with one another. Nobody is going anywhere. We're here, side by side. You might as well move up to category two so we can win, not lose, as a nation.

Our two political parties try to divide our country to win elections. The Democrats go after the black and brown vote. Republicans go after the white vote. Then each professes to be distraught and uncomprehending when we don't unite after the election. They try to win by playing to fear and suspicion. Then they try to govern by being gentler and kinder.

The melting pot is our strength, not our weakness. Our culture is dynamic because it is varied. Our nation became the envy of the world because it is a unique tapestry woven of many strands drawn from every part of the globe.

I am not closing my eyes to the real world. I realize that some groups have advantages and that others have disadvantages, but we don't pull anyone up by pulling somebody else down. We're all in the same boat, and we will sink or sail together.

The law must be color-blind. Justice must be color-blind.

Where there are disadvantages, we must put our brains and our resources into helping people overcome them. In Chapter Five, I said we must put a ladder down into the worst areas of our inner cities. We must lend a hand in making sure children are able to reach the first rung on that ladder. This is the kind of affirmative action that works. We don't need to promote less qualified people over more qualified people. What we need is more qualified people. If we're to compete effectively, we need millions of more qualified people.

Unless we repair our economy, those who are down can expect to stay down. We need to repair our job-creating engine. That's where we need to direct our energies. The NAACP should make it a goal to make black smallbusiness owners heroes to their neighbors. These are the ladder builders for the next generation.

This is not the problem of one community. It is a problem for our country, and we can turn it into an opportunity for our country. Our commitment must be to become one team again. On a team every member contributes. Only a team intent on losing tells some of its members to sit on the sidelines. We need to bring everyone off the bench and on to the field. Whatever it takes, we should do it. In the long run it's the only way we are all going to win.

A Nation Working Together

If you're pro-life, think over my position, then ask a friend who is pro-choice to read it and think it over. Then discuss it together. Can't we do more to solve this problem by working together than by fighting one another? What more could we do? You two talk it over. Start with where you agree. We already know where you disagree.

AN AMERICA THAT HEALS

If you're white, read my position here and in Chapter Five. Show it to friends who are black or Hispanic or Asian, and ask them to think it over. Is it enough? What more can we do? Argue over it. This is the kind of open, positive debate we've avoided for too long. We shouldn't be embarrassed to talk about race. We've tried to sweep these problems under the rug for so long the floor has risen a couple of inches. It's time to talk to one another.

We cannot expect our political leaders to lead where the people will not follow. However, it seems to me that the people are ready and willing to put these divisions behind us. Since these issues are also enmeshed in government policy, we should demand that our candidates for public offices undertake the moral responsibility of helping us to heal.

CHAPTER SEVEN

An America that Leads

W hat does America stand for? Only a few years ago we were the exemplar of nations. America set the pace for the world in inventiveness, in creating jobs, in raising living standards. Abroad, we shaped the trading and monetary systems as master of a smooth-running economy, as custodians of a strong currency and as financiers of the world. Our economic might underwrote peace and prosperity. It provided the military strength to repel Soviet threats to democracy. It provided for the resurrection of the great nations in Europe and the Pacific. It became the global engine of reform, of growth, of hope for the future.

The world once looked to us with wonder. Now they look at us *and* wonder. Foreign leaders are alarmed by our runaway debt, our social problems, our failing educational system. They express chagrin, and sometimes even contempt, at our political leadership.

Only an economically strong United States can preserve world peace, promote democracy, encourage expanding markets, and serve as a beacon of promise for the potential of mankind.

Start at Home

Our highest foreign-policy priority is to get our house in order and make America work again. This is not isolationism or nationalism. It is common sense. The world needs a strong, purposeful United States. We cannot lead others or be a reliable partner if we are weak and divided at home. Getting the American house in order is the point of departure for a new American foreign policy.

Second, we must realize that far too many of our foreign policy structures are based on doctrines of the 1940s. They are old and out of date. We need to create new structures for the 1990s and the new century. That means changing a lot of things. We must restructure the White House staff and the organization of the state and defense departments. We must update our security arrangements and rethink overseas deployments. We must reform the alphabet soup of international agencies we have put in place over the past fifty years to deal with the world that used to be—from the UN to NATO, GATT, IMF, and the World Bank.

We have much to change to provide for a foreign policy in keeping with the needs of the world that *is,* rather than the world that *was*. Too much taxpayer money and administrative effort is being needlessly consumed by outdated policies and outdated structures.

Emphasize Trade

For far too long, Washington has maintained an artificial distinction between domestic and international policy. The "high" politics of defense and diplomacy has received too much attention at the expense of the "low" politics of the economy and jobs. To succeed in the world of today, we must view domestic and foreign policy in terms of a single, interwoven net of national interests.

America's position in the world today depends as much on the productivity of our labor and the performance of our schools as it does on the number of missiles in our arsenal. At the same time we cannot achieve our goals of rebuilding our country without having trade and financial cooperation with other nations.

Trade means jobs. Fair and equitable trade means more jobs. Jobs mean a higher standard of living, a healthier economy and a lower deficit. That produces a stronger America that can buy more from our allies. An American policy of fair and equitable trade is good for all nations.

We must be frank about our trade position. It cannot be improved by making excuses or berating others who outcompete us.

Too often, our political and business leaders seem to respond only by complaining. They whine and bluster. That's the response of losers.

It's time that Americans responded like winners. We should replace the political appointees who are sent from Washington to fail to negotiate advantageous agreements. We need to put in their place experienced, hard-nosed negotiators from outside politics who know how to achieve good deals.

We need to learn from the Japanese and the Europeans. They are not our enemies. They are our allies. However, they are tough competitors. We just have to get our act together so that we can outcompete them fair and square. Also, we have to negotiate harder. The Europeans and the Japanese outnegotiate us at every turn in trade talks.

Get Moving in the Pacific

To the Japanese, I would say this: we will get our house in order as you and all our allies have suggested. In turn, we demand that you share more fully in keeping the world safe for future generations.

You must shoulder more of the burden of stationing U.S. troops and ships in your region. You must cooperate with us on the environment, on rebuilding the former Soviet Union, in multinational peacekeeping efforts, in defusing nuclear risks, in sharing in the burden of handling refugees, and in creating conditions for global economic growth, including in the United States. We can no longer accept the excuse that the Japanese are unique or different. We are all citizens of the world.

Elsewhere in the Pacific, we must pursue markets aggressively. The USA is as economically integrated into the Pacific as Germany is in the European Community. Japan is our second largest trading partner. Beyond Japan are China, Korea, and other Asian countries. All told, we trade 30 percent more across the Pacific than we do across the Atlantic. The Asian/ Pacific region is the fastest growing sector of the world economy. If we are smart, we can sell a lot of American products there. We must place a high emphasis on penetrating the vast markets of the Pacific basin.

China deserves special attention as a remaining bastion of communism. The present administration has spent its time coddling a geriatric central government when the real action is taking place in the provinces. Beijing still may be playing the old communist song, but the provinces are dancing to capitalist tunes. While we talk to a deaf leadership, free markets are developing all across the country. They have solid examples close at hand. Hong Kong is already the tenth largest economy in the world. Taiwan has the largest foreign exchange reserves in the world. The 63 million people of Guangdong Province are becoming voracious consumers. We must construct a diplomacy that deals with the complexity of this vast land and advances an agenda of democracy. Someone once said that free markets produce free minds. Through a concerted policy of engagement we can help the Chinese people attain their goals of political liberty and democratic institutions. Once open to free trade, a door can't be shut to free thought.

We must also begin thinking of new ways to share the burden of maintaining peace in the Pacific. At present, the security of the region is maintained by five security agreements that we maintain under bilateral agreements. There is no collective security device like NATO in the Pacific.

It will take perhaps a generation, if not more, to devise collective security measures that encompass cultures as different as Japan and China, India and Indonesia. We must begin discussions now. Unlike the current administration, the next one must think more progressively on this front.

Build on Success in Europe

We must nurture our successes across the Atlantic. NATO is the most successful military alliance in history. Yet we must not hang on to NATO just for the sake of preserving a venerable institution. It is time to develop a successor mechanism.

There are risks in Europe. All is not milk and honey there. That said, Europeans are better equipped than ever to manage those risks.

We can no longer make the argument that U.S. forces are needed in Europe to provide frontline protection of the United States.

We cannot justify using U.S. taxpayers' money to station troops on German soil to protect Western Europe from potential intra-European strife. The Europeans—thanks in part to our presence for the past 45 years—have the ability to do this themselves. Everyone is aware of the age-old tensions that occasionally raise their ugly heads in Europe. Keeping U.S. troops on European soil to ward off those historical impulses in the age of democracy is akin to a parent leaving a light on in a child's room at night to ward off ghosts. It is hard to justify "night light" troops at U.S. taxpayer expense.

We will not withdraw completely from Europe. We

will stand ready to come to the aid of our European allies. However, we want them to take the lead and bear the lion's share of the burden in providing for their own security.

The former Soviet Union presents an unusual burden and a special responsibility for the United States and the rest of the world. The breakup of the Soviet empire is fraught with risks. Nationalism and ethnic strife are inevitable consequences of the unwinding of artificial geographic and cultural arrangements imposed by Stalin and his successors. There is potential for nuclear mischief. There is a real danger that reform will fail.

My policy toward the Commonwealth of Independent States would be to work both unilaterally and closely with the Europeans, the Japanese, and collective agencies like the U.N. to:

1. Put nuclear warheads out of commission wherever they are. Our negotiators continue to concentrate on missile delivery systems, a vestige of Cold War arms control. The warheads are the primary threat. We cannot rest until all warheads in the four nuclear CIS states are accounted for and under control;

2. Contain any imperialistic tendencies harbored by any of the former Soviet territories;

3. Send appropriate aid, technology, support personnel, and other items needed to build a bulwark for liberty. Make sure the channels are established to administer our help effectively, instead of allowing it to be wasted by state enterprises or poorly conceived projects.

Work with Latin America

The failure of Soviet communism has put an end to Leninist imitators in the American hemisphere. Castro is the sole holdout in this part of the world. We must continue to isolate Castro. Elsewhere in Latin America we must continue to encourage the transition to market capitalism. We are profiting from the democratization and privatization of Latin economies. This is largely because we are the leading producer of goods used to build nations, like telephone switches, trucks and aircraft.

American exports to South America grew 20 percent last year. Jobs are being created to fill those orders. I want to make sure that this expansion of American jobs continues. I want to make sure it is not a temporary thing. This is why I want to examine the Mexican trade agreement closely.

This trade agreement presents an exciting opportunity for both our nations. I applaud the tremendous progress the Mexican government has made under President Salinas in revitalizing a tired, socialized economy. In five years Mexico has privatized 75 percent of its state-run enterprises. Always a deservedly proud nation, Mexico has earned the admiration of the world.

Challenges remain. In Mexico, workers are paid between one and two dollars an hour. Environmental and pollution regulations are laxly enforced. Health care for workers is rarely provided. The challenge is to create a trade agreement that helps Mexico to continue to pull itself up but that does not pull us down. I do not want a trade agreement that trades away jobs. I want a trade agreement that creates good paying permanent jobs on both sides of the border.

I fully understand why our own Hispanic community so strongly supports trade ties with Mexico. This community is a marvelous resource with its ability to act as a bridge between two dynamic cultures. We should commit to putting that bridge in place and make sure the road over it runs both ways.

Achieve Peace in Africa and the Middle East

On the other side of the world, Africa must not be neglected. Once treated as pawns by the two superpowers, the undeveloped countries of the sub-Sahara region now have the best opportunity in the post-colonial era to establish independent democratic institutions and free markets. Already the most prosperous nation on the continent, South Africa deserves American support as it makes a successful transition to true democracy and sheds the shameful vestiges of apartheid. Together with the Europeans and Asians, we must work hard to see that democratization succeeds in South Africa and that lasting economic progress finally takes root in the sub-Sahara region of the continent.

For the past fifty years, United States policy in the Middle East has been geared to preventing the area from falling under control of any power that might threaten our vital interests. During the Cold War, the Soviet Union and local governments acting as its agent were of particular concern to us. Today, we must remain vigilant against actions of other powers whose interests in the region are opposed to ours.

Since its founding as a nation, Israel has been our staunchest ally in the region. Our support for an Israel secure from external threat goes beyond the noble sentiment of friendship. Israel is of strategic importance to the United States. During the Cold War, she was a bulwark against Soviet aggression in the Middle East. In the aftermath of the Cold War, Israel is a beacon of democracy in a region populated largely by dictatorships and monarchies. We must remain committed to the continued defense and support of Israel militarily, diplomatically, and financially in order to secure the prospect for democracy in the region.

Israel's long-term security and overall stability in the Middle East depends on the successful resolution of an Arab-Israeli peace agreement from which all parties benefit. We must continue to work tirelessly with all governments of the region to reach a lasting peace.

Don't Encourage Tyrants

While we now have the luxury of defining our foreign policy needs largely in economic terms, we must remember that there are still military threats to our nation's security. The world of the 1990s is unfortunately populated by brilliant, psychotic despots who are not against cannibalizing civilization to advance their own agendas. The list is well known—Saddam in Iraq, Qaddafi in Libya, Assad in Syria, Kim in North Korea, and Castro in Cuba. This list may be tragically expanded by renegade forces in the former Soviet territories if chaos ensues.

We should follow consistent policies toward rogue governments. I would treat outlaws for what they are. Where America's vital interests are not impacted, I expect others to take the lead in containing these renegades, with our support. The UN and other collective agencies must be involved. We should reserve the right, in consultation with Congress, to take into our own muscular hands any rogue government that threatens vital American interests.

The most effective way to deal with criminal states is not to encourage them in the first place. If we don't like brutal third world dictators, we shouldn't help create another one. We supported General Noriega. We sent him weapons, millions of dollars, and flattering letters. We inflated him until his ego ballooned out of control. It now turns out that we were doing the same thing with Saddam Hussein. These cases didn't just cost us money. They cost us something far more precious: the lives of American soldiers.

We could have avoided all this if we had followed Winston Churchill's simple advice: "Never cozy up with tyrants. They'll always turn on you."

Demand a New Vision

The world is at a crucial turning point in history. We must seize the moment and turn frightful risks into great opportunities. Just as we must embrace bold programs to repair our economy, our cities and our schools, we must move bravely on the world stage. The American people should demand more of their presidential candidates than debates on the fine points of diplomacy. They should insist that each candidate provide a vision of a new architecture for a new world. They should demand blueprints for action.

When he was suddenly faced with the opportunity to make the Louisiana Purchase, Thomas Jefferson didn't take a poll. He acted.

When he was confronted by the devastation of Western Europe after the war, Harry Truman didn't hesitate. He acted.

An American President is supposed to be able to see past the moment. He should be able to see history in the making. He should be capable for shaping history in America's interest.

That is the standard by which our Presidents should be measured.

Afterword

The Perot phenomenon that swept the country through the spring and summer of 1992 had little to do with me. It was a spontaneous grassroots outpouring that has transformed a deep-seated concern with our political system into a positive citizen movement for reform.

Others campaigning for office will try to capitalize on your efforts. A person doesn't become a politician without learning how to dance the two-step. I hope many of them will do more than try to play to the crowd. I hope they will listen to the roar of the crowd. Those who don't, or who try to get by with the two-step, should be defeated.

I'm talking about all of our elected officials who have allowed this great system to be mired in the mud of special interests, who have padded themselves with perks at our expense, and who have rigged the election system to avoid answering to the people.

We don't need term limits as long as we have the ballot. If in this upcoming election we demand that candidates face up to the real issues that confront us, you can be sure that after the election members of the House and Senate will continue to listen to this country's owners. The reforms we so desperately need will be enacted quickly. That's the glory of our Constitution. Our elected officials listen, or they become former officials.

AFTERWORD

The grassroots movement that put me on the ballot in state after state has sent a message too strong to ignore. Volunteers did it, and they did it without the support of any established party, any political machine, or any special interest group. That amazing achievement has already jolted the political establishment. The little group of Washington insiders, lobbyists, and professional politicians who thought of the national government as their own private playground are waking up to the fact that this country doesn't belong to them.

The Appendix has a list of topics important to this country. All the candidates need to know that you care about these issues and that you will vote according to their positions on them. Ask the candidates what they will do about the items on the list. Remember what they say. Hold them accountable once they're elected.

There are five principles which animated this movement from the beginning and which will carry it through Election Day and beyond. These principles are the themes that underlie this book. I hope they will someday underlie the governing of this country.

One. The people are the owners of this country. Everyone in government, from the President of the United States to the newest employee in a small town, works for the people.

Two. All of us must take personal responsibility for our actions and for the actions of our government. Citizenship in the United States is a privilege that can only be safeguarded by its exercise.

Three. We are a single team. The task ahead is enormous. We are all needed in the rebuilding of America.

Four. We can't keep living beyond our means. The size of government must be permanently reduced. The deficit must be eliminated. We can handle shared sacrifice. We cannot survive an irresponsible government.

Five. Our greatest challenge is economic competition. Our governmental policies should be redirected to stimulate growth, to encourage the private sector, to create jobs, and to open opportunities for all Americans.

* * *

Alexis de Tocqueville crossed the Atlantic in 1831 to observe the growing power called the United States. He summed up his two-volume study by saying, "America is great because its people are good." Nothing has changed. I saw this in the last several months by working with thousands of people from all walks of life. America's strength is its people. You are deeply patriotic, creative, and dedicated. You are filled with love for your country. You are brimming with ideas. You are determined to leave a better country to your children. You are at one with the spirit of our forefathers.

When the Founders signed the Declaration of Independence, they pledged their lives, their fortunes, and their sacred honor. They were deadly serious in making that pledge. When they picked up the quill pen to place their names on that document, they did so with the certain knowledge that it could cost them their lives.

AFTERWORD

One signer, John Hart, was driven from the bedside of his dying wife by an English patrol sent to capture him. His thirteen children scattered and fled for their lives. He lived in the fields and the forests and in caves, eluding the enemy, until the end of the war. When he returned home, his wife was dead, his house was burnt to the ground, his farm was destroyed, and his children were nowhere to be found. A few weeks later he died from exhaustion and a broken heart.

Compared to that, what are the minor sacrifices we are called upon to make to pull our nation out of bankruptcy, to restore our spirit, and to put America on a new course for our children's future?

Our political leaders have been afraid to ask those sacrifices of the American people. This is one more case where the people see more clearly than the leaders do. The people have rightly resisted minor adjustments, knowing that the hands writing the laws were being guided by special interests seeking preference for one group over another. They are crying out for a plan like the one laid out in this book that distributes the burden carefully on all but the weakest shoulders so that together we can pull this nation out of the mire. We can no longer expect our political leaders to have the strength or the courage to do it. Only the people can give them the power.

Only the people can keep faith with our forefathers. We owe everything we have to them. Today in India or Ecuador or Togo there are people who are as bright, as capable, and as ambitious as any of us. They will never have the chance to do something great with their marvelous talents. No matter how smart or able they are, they will never have the opportunity because they weren't born in the country our forefathers founded.

Only the people can keep faith with those who have already sacrificed so much for our country. I didn't make the navy my career. Many of my classmates at the Naval Academy did. Some of them died defending our country. Some of them spent years of their lives in prison camps, never bending an inch in devotion to our country. I went into business. Most of you went to school, raised a family, entered a profession, or got a good-paying job. They could have gone that same route, but they didn't. They served their country.

Only the people can keep faith with our fathers and mothers. Mario Cuomo's father worked his way to these shores and worked at menial jobs until he was able to bring over his wife and children. Today his son is the governor of New York. Other more established families lost everything in the Great Depression. Some mothers and fathers who were people of distinction and achievement went to work as fieldhands to keep their children fed and clothed. Some scraped enough money together so at least one child could go to college. The sacrifices made by that generation compose one of the brightest chapters of nobility in the annals of human history.

Only the people can keep faith with our children. In the 1960s, our standard of living doubled every generation and a half. Parents who worked on a farm could send a child to college and live to see their grandchildren build successful businesses. At our present low growth rate, it will take twelve generations for our standard of living to double. The children of a child born this year will be dead before our standard of living doubles again.

AFTERWORD

We have broken the faith we owe to our children. The politicians can't restore it. Only the people can.

Only the people, the owners of this country, can make America strong again.

The Founders believed in the people. They knew in their hearts and souls that each generation would have to work to pass on a greater nation to the next generation.

Only the people can remake our country.

Time is short. History is merciless. The whole world waits for your decision.

Appendix

Check List for All Federal Candidates

We would like to have your specific plans to:

———— Eliminate the deficit
———— Keep the budget balanced through binding legislation
———— Pay off the national debt
———— Rebuild the job base and put our people back to work
———— Develop an intelligent, supportive relationship between government and business
———— Develop strategic plans industry by industry to strengthen and rebuild our companies
———— Target the industries of the future and develop specific plans to be the world leader in those industries
———— Stimulate the growth of small businesses
———— Maintain and build our manufacturing base
———— Make "Made in the USA" the world's standard of excellence
———— Rebuild our cities
———— Make our public schools the finest in the world
———— Get rid of illegal drugs
———— Dramatically reduce crime and violence throughout our country
———— Provide affordable health care
———— Get rid of waste, fraud, and abuse in the federal government

APPENDIX

——— Develop a new tax system that is fair, paperless for most Americans, and raises the money necessary to pay our country's bills

——— Get rid of foreign lobbyists and foreign political contributions

——— Develop *fair* free-trade agreements

——— Pass laws prohibiting cashing in on prior government service

——— Develop an intelligent energy policy

——— Implement the line item veto for the President

——— Pass laws to stop Congress from exempting itself from laws it imposes on the rest of the country

——— Bring the congressional retirement plan in line with private-sector plans

——— Pass laws requiring the return of all excess campaign funds to the U.S. Treasury

——— Pass laws to reduce the time for federal elections, reduce the cost of federal campaigns, and create equal opportunity for all new candidates by providing equal television time for all candidates

——— Replace the electoral college with the popular vote

——— Pass laws eliminating all possibilities for special interests to give large sums of money to candidates

——— Pass a law to hold elections on Saturday and Sunday, instead of Tuesday

——— Pass a law forbidding release of election information before the polls in Hawaii close

——— Slash staffs in the executive and legislative branches

——— Get rid of unnecessary perks throughout the federal government